THE MAGIC & MYSTERY OF
IRELAND

Biographies and Acknowledgements

Bill Doyle was born in Dublin and has lived there all his life. His interest in photography
started many years ago, with a hill-walking expedition to the islands with his camera, and
this was followed in 1967 by a *Daily Telegraph Magazine* award for photography. Since then he
has dedicated his time to capturing all aspects of Irish life, culture and landscape in pictures.

For Mia
Sonya Newland's love of Ireland developed after seeing photographs of the outstanding Irish
countryside. She lives in London but makes regular visits to Ireland, fuelling a love of Irish
literature, particularly the poetry of Yeats.

With grateful thanks to Helen Courtney who designed this book and to Kelley Doak.

All pictures courtesy of Bill Doyle except as follows:
pages 14, 29, 31, 33, 35, 64, 67, 90, 102, 172, 179 courtesy of the Northern Ireland Tourist Board
pages 18, 21, 24, 32, 167 © Dept. of Arts, Heritage, Gaeltacht & the Islands
page 197 courtesy of The Bridgeman Art Library

ISBN 1-84084-010-2

This is a Dempsey Parr Book
This edition published in 2000
Dempsey Parr is an imprint of Parragon
Parragon, Queen Street House, 4 Queen Street, Bath BA1 1HE

Copyright © Parragon 1998

Produced for Dempsey Parr by Foundry Design and Production,
Crabtree Hall, Crabtree Lane, Fulham, London SW6 6TY.

THE MAGIC & MYSTERY OF
IRELAND

PHOTOGRAPHS BY BILL DOYLE

Text by Sonya Newland

DP

DEMPSEY
PARR

Contents

Contents *by* Region

Introduction

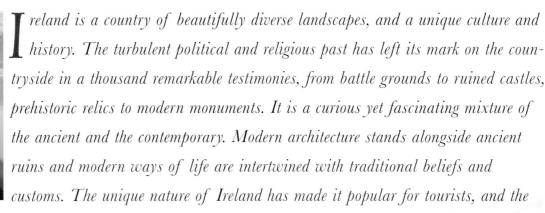

Ireland is a country of beautifully diverse landscapes, and a unique culture and history. The turbulent political and religious past has left its mark on the countryside in a thousand remarkable testimonies, from battle grounds to ruined castles, prehistoric relics to modern monuments. It is a curious yet fascinating mixture of the ancient and the contemporary. Modern architecture stands alongside ancient ruins and modern ways of life are intertwined with traditional beliefs and customs. The unique nature of Ireland has made it popular for tourists, and the breathtaking beauty of the countryside, together with the unquenchable enthusiasm for life and fun that seems to be an integral part of the Irish nature have made it a haven for both young and old, those seeking peace and solitude, and those in search of more energetic activities.

It is nearly impossible to travel anywhere in Ireland without stumbling across tangible reminders of the rich and varied history of the country. Although it seems that Ireland's past is a patchwork of battles and revolutions, antagonism and retribution, the history of this nation is in fact an extraordinary tale of social and cultural development that dates back to prehistoric times.

The first people came across to Ireland around 8000 years BC, before the rising sea isolated it from the mainland of Scotland, but only a few rare stone tools serve as reminders of this civilisation. Over one thousand years later, they were followed by another group who travelled across the narrow channel that then separated Ireland from Scotland, and they lived here undisturbed for over 3000 years. Eventually, a new band of people

began to move into Ireland from countries further afield, and it was these Neolithic people who left the first lasting legacies of their time, including the fantastic dolmen, ancient tombs and many other relics of pagan rites and worship that are still scattered around the countryside. From this time, there was steady influx of new inhabitants to Ireland, including the Celts, who remain the most influential of Ireland's early races. They had strong social and religious beliefs and practices, and much Celtic jewellery and metalwork has been discovered that has shown the Celts to be an artistic as well as a fierce and courageous race of people. The Celts fought and ruled in Ireland for over 1000 years.

St Patrick, the country's Patron Saint came to Ireland in the fifth century, and succeeded in spreading the word of Christianity to the inhabitants. By the following century, Ireland reached its height of Christian affluence and power, dominated by successful monastic settlements that were major centres of learning and discovery, of scholarship and prayer. This time of peace and opulence did not last long: in AD 795 the Vikings invaded the Irish coasts and islands and continued to move further inland, making raids on the mainland settlements. They were eventually overthrown in the famous Battle of Clontarf, which took place near Dublin in 1014. It was during this battle that the renowned King Brian Boru was killed.

After this time the churches were handed back to the monastic orders, many churches and monasteries that had been attacked and destroyed were rebuilt, and there was a revival of the old religious practices and worship. In 1169, however, the country was invaded by the infamous Norman knight Richard de Clare and his armies, who seized Dublin and proceeded to take over much of Ireland. The wars between the Celts and the Normans raged for over 300 years. In 1541, Henry VIII was acknowledged as the king of

Ireland, and the great period of Catholic suppression began, during which many of the great monastic settlements in Ireland were again destroyed. This was continued with a vengeance by his daughter Elizabeth I, whose armies fought bitterly to assert her Protestant reformation in the country, and by the time of James I, English law was proclaimed the law of the land, and the native Irish had been taken off their land, and replaced by English Protestants. There followed a period of great affluence in Ireland, that was broken only by the Great Famine of the mid-1800s.

The total failure of the potato crops caused over one million Irish people to die from starvation and disease. Those that lived fled the country mostly to North America, from fear of a similar fate. The result was that the population of the country dropped to less than half its pre-famine numbers. This tragedy led to an increased demand for freedom from English rule. Led by Charles Stuart Parnell, a campaign for 'Home Rule' was started. The Easter Rising of 1916 forged the way, finally gaining a hearing for the

people of Ireland, and the Irish Treaty of 1921 granted independence to the Irish Free State, while Britain retained control of the northern counties of the country. Ireland was a divided nation.

From pre-Christian times, the Irish peoples and races have left their marks all over the landscape, buried deep within the hillsides, leering dangerously on cliff-edges, tucked away in mountain slopes and standing proudly in fields all over the country. The oldest, and perhaps the most eerily impressive are the ancient standing stones, dolmens and stone circles that pervade the hillsides. They are spell-binding relics of a time before Christianity reached the island, and they reveal a little about the fascinating rituals and beliefs that formed the basis of their civilisation. More frequently, though, they bring to mind the mysteries that remain unsolved about these people. How did they construct such monoliths as the Poulnabrone or Browne's Hill dolmen, and what exactly was their purpose?

The legacy of the early Christian era is the largest and most widespread through-out the country. There are many monasteries, abbeys, churches and other examples of the time of Christian affluence around, in various states of ruin. The wealth of these monuments makes Ireland unique. Almost everywhere you turn, you stumble across an ancient ruin of some description. Many of these are still dedicated to the saints who founded them – or

in whose honour they were founded – many centuries ago, and they are still sites of pilgrimage and homage. Set in remote and beautiful parts of the country, many of the medieval monastic sites, such as the one at Glendalough in Co. Wicklow are both exceptionally beautiful, and thought-provoking in their sadly decimated splendour.

The other famous monuments of this era are the Celtic high crosses. The familiar ringed cross set on a heavy base and often with marvellous and intricate engravings, are not confined to just the sites of old churches and monasteries, but are an integral part of the Irish landscape, becoming in themselves a symbol of Ireland. Besides these, there is a wealth of relics in the form of castles and forts. The most

abundant of these were built by the Normans, and they are especially prominent along the coastal cliffs. These are an awe-inspiring testimony to the endurance of this race that fought so bitterly for dominance in Ireland for many centuries.

The more recent architecture found in the cities and towns of Ireland is also impressive. The affluence of the eighteenth century can be seen in the grandiose styles of many great country houses throughout both Northern and Southern Ireland, and in many of the official buildings that stand in the country's capital, Dublin. The great architect James Gandon was responsible for a number of the magnificent structures that stand along the waters of the River Liffey, including the Four Courts and the Custom House. All these relics, from the most ancient to the most recent, are a magnificent reflection of the country's natural beauty and majesty.

Ireland's climate is renowned for its unpredictability. The weather can, quite literally, change dramatically from one minute to the next. Its naturally moist air, and warm gulf-stream climate have created a land that is lush and green, earning it the well-deserved title of the 'Emerald Isle'. There are miles and miles of open fields and pastures, where agriculture is still one of the main industries of the island. Yet side by side with this, there are vast expanses of bald, formidable limestone rocks and crags. The many mountain ranges in Ireland dominate the landscapes, in a rich array of blues and purples, and there are undiscovered paths still amidst their peaks. It is a climber's paradise. The lowlands are often characterised by bog lands, where peat is still mined for everyday fuel. The coastal areas, now increasingly popular with tourists, remain spectacular, breathtaking scenes of sheer cliffs dropping to a violent and pounding ocean, or – in this land of contrasts – calm, beautiful stretches of sand that shimmer like opals. Each of the islands off the shores of the country has its own unique traditions and customs, like many of the mainland areas. Many areas are still Gaelic-speaking, and one can still catch a glimpse of the Ireland of past generations.

It is a land of magical scenery and a mysterious past. There are secrets locked in the land that will never be discovered, and there is magic to be discovered in almost every wooded glen, or mountain peak. In no other country in the world does the soul of the nation shine through with such obvious brilliance in the landscape, climate, architecture, lifestyle, and most importantly, the Irish people themselves.

RELICS FROM THE PAST

From mysterious pagan statues to resplendent medieval castles, almost every county in Ireland has a wealth of relics that have survived the ages to tell the tale of ancient times and historic peoples.

Gosford Castle
CO. ARMAGH

This impressive, sprawling castle stands in the middle of Gosford Forest Park, near Markethill in Co. Armagh. The building replaced a manor house that once stood on this spot. It is in fact a mock Norman castle, built in imitation of the great strongholds that the Normans erected in Ireland throughout the thirteenth and fourteenth centuries. All over the country, ruins of original Norman castles, towers and forts can be seen.

Like many of these, Gosford Castle comprises a square keep, and a round tower built of stone. It gives a good indication of how these buildings would once have looked, now that most are in ruins, destroyed by wars and time. The building was designed by Thomas Hopper in 1818, and is set amongst acres of beautiful park land and landscaped gardens. It was originally the estate of the Earls of Gosford, but since its construction it has been used for many purposes, including as a military base during World War II. Gosford Castle is a fine relic of the more recent past, and an appropriate reflection of the medieval history of the country.

Oranmore Castle
CO. GALWAY

The village of Oranmore lies at the central point of the roads leading to Galway, Dublin, Killarney and Sligo, and this has made it a popular place for visitors, particularly those passing through to the bustling county town of Galway. Oranmore itself is a relatively quiet, picturesque village at the heart of the oyster country, on the shores of Galway Bay.

The air of tranquillity that pervades the village now, however, gives no indication of its past. In ancient times the area surrounding Oranmore was dominated by medieval invaders, and relics of these more turbulent times lie scattered in the countryside for miles outside the village. These include ruined forts, castles, and a round tower, as well as more ancient relics such as stone dolmens. In later times this part of the country became popular for its ideal location and peaceful scenery, and began to see a number of large country houses springing up.

The fifteenth-century castle at Oranmore stands silhouetted against the sunset over Galway Bay, a natural part of the stunning evening landscape. These typical, square Norman-built forts are a familiar sight along the coastlines of districts such as this, and are a silent memorial to the country's tumultuous past.

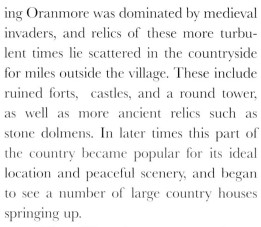

Tower at Liscannor
CO. CLARE

Standing vigil on the cliff edge at Liscannor in Co. Clare, this ruined castle tower has been here since the fifteenth century. It was one of many towers built along this line of the coast as a look-out point, and as fortification against an expected invasion from Spain – an attack that never came. Many of these towers and forts have disappeared completely, but the remains of a few can still be seen dotted along the cliff edges. Today, they can offer magnificent views out to sea, stretching for many miles to a horizon that has remained unchanged since the first look-outs were posted here all those centuries ago.

The castle lies on the edge of the village of Liscannor, a relatively undisturbed place, which gains its fame from being the home town of John Holland, the man who invented the submarine. In keeping with the Irish patriotism, and fervent defence of their country's independence, Holland worked on his invention in the United States, with the intention of using it in the US fleet to help destroy the British. There is a plaque in the picturesque harbour to commemorate his achievement.

Jerpoint Abbey
CO. KILKENNY

The magnificent remains of Jerpoint Abbey lie just south of Thomastown in Co. Kilkenny. Built in 1160, the abbey was originally intended for the Benedictine monks, but it was taken over just twenty years later by a Cistercian order from Baltinglass Abbey. Jerpoint remained home to the Cistercian monks and brothers for over 350 years. During this period the building was expanded, adding the cloisters and a crossing tower to the parts that were already there, these included a church, kitchens, stables and also its own cemetery, infirmary and gardens. With the dissolution of the monasteries in 1540, possession of the abbey passed to the Earl of Ormonde who leased it from the English king.

Although much of the abbey is now destroyed, it remains a fascinating Irish landmark. The Romanesque carvings in the nave are still visible, and the cloisters, although perhaps the most badly damaged by the ravages of time, still boast many sculptures reflecting the chivalry of the age in which the abbey flourished: knights and dragons, ladies fair and courtly scenes. The tombs that remain — most of them sixteenth century — also possess exquisite carvings of saints, bishops and other religious figures.

Ruins at Ullard
CO. KILKENNY

The ruins of an old church stand at Ullard, not far away from the ancient town of Graiguenamanagh. This area of Kilkenny is home to a wealth of ancient sites, including an early monastic settlement, believed to have been founded by St Fiacra, with a splendid granite cross depicting the figures of Adam and Eve, and the Twelve Apostles amongst other more ambiguous carvings.

This striking doorway is typical of the Romanesque style of carving that characterises so many of these ancient sites. The Romanesque fashion took its influences from the French churches, probably brought to Ireland by pilgrims, and the first Romanesque churches are likely to have been built in honour of the saints who founded them.

The ornate carvings typical of the style were usually restricted to certain areas of the church and abbey buildings, mainly doorways and gables. They range from fairly simple motifs and symbols, through more complicated, interlaced twists and knots, to beautifully ornate, intricate patterns. The most advanced Romanesque carvings detail faces fashioned from stone that stare impressively from the archways over main entrances and doorways.

Round Tower at Kilmacduagh
CO. GALWAY

The remains of the large Augustinian monastic settlement at Kilmacduagh stand in isolation on the borders of Co. Clare and Co. Galway. This site was founded in the seventh century by St Colman MacDuagh, but is likely to have undergone some restoration during the eleventh century, when there was a revival of monastic power and affluence.

The most impressive monument that remains here is the imposing round tower, standing undaunted against the blue skies of Galway. This has survived much better than the other buildings on the site – despite its distinctive but precarious tilt. Round towers were built on most monastic sites and enjoyed a number of uses. They were primarily intended as places of safety in the event of attack, and were designed with this in mind – with an elevated entrance accessed by a ladder that would be hauled up once the monks and brothers were all safely inside. In times of peace and prosperity, they were used largely as store-houses for the beautiful manuscripts created by the monks, which were extremely valuable.

St Kevin's Church
CO. WICKLOW

St Kevin founded a hermitage in the serene Glendalough ('Glen of the Two Lakes') in the sixth century. His reputation for piety, however, soon caused many others to be drawn to this place and eventually a monastery was built to accommodate the increasing numbers. Here, in the solitude of this beautiful area, the monks and brothers flourished, to such an extent that the place became an entire monastic city.

After St Kevin's death in AD 619 (he is reputed to have lived to the age of 120), the settlement continued to prosper, but harder times were on the way. Plundered by the Vikings in the ninth and tenth centuries, and flooded in the twelfth century, many of the buildings were practically destroyed. The English attack on nearby Dublin saw further destruction in 1389, and the settlement finally disappeared in the conquest of Wicklow during the fifteenth and sixteenth centuries.

Despite this, parts of the monastery still survive, as well as several churches, the cathedral and an impressive round tower. The site remained a centre of pilgrimage for many years after, and is still a popular attraction, not least because of the many fascinating myths and legends that surround the enigmatic St Kevin.

Monastery at Dysert O'Dea
CO. CLARE

The monastic site at Dysert O'Dea is believed to have been founded in the eighth century by St Tola, but little is really known about this ancient settlement. It is a wild, overgrown ruin that carries echoes of the past through its ravaged stonework and grassy courtyards. Most of the main buildings have been worn away by time, but fortunately some of the fascinating carvings that would have appeared throughout the buildings have survived. One of the most beautiful of these is pictured here – a marvellous Romanesque carving that features many ancient faces peering out over one of the doorways.

Not far away is the site of the great battle of Dysert O'Dea, where the Englishman Richard de Clare and his army attacked Conor O'Dea in 1318. It was a fierce and bloody battle, and was won by the O'Deas with the support of other Irish clans such as the O'Connors and the famous O'Briens. For more than two hundred years following this battle, the English lost their supremacy in Clare, and the O'Deas built a stronghold there in the fifteenth century to prevent further attacks. The remains of this fort still stand.

The Rock of Cashel
CO. TIPPERARY

Throughout the hundreds of years since it was first built, the incredible stone fort of Cashel has seen both bloody battles and times of prosperity, been home to kings and churchmen, and played host to some of Ireland's most famous historic figures.

For nearly a millennium, from the fourth century, this stone stronghold was the seat of the kings of Munster, the Eoghanachta. This dynasty struggled for dominance over the whole of Ireland, and their seat extended to much of the southern part of the country. The infamous Brian Boru was crowned king here in AD 977.

In 1101 Muircheartach O'Brien handed the Rock of Cashel over to the Church, and it was a flourishing religious centre until the Cromwellian army attacked it in 1647, killing all its thousands of inhabitants. Throughout this history, the Rock was extended and developed: a chapel and round tower were added in the early twelfth century, and a thirteenth century cathedral remains the most impressive monument still standing on the Rock. Cashel is one of the most well-preserved and fascinating of all Ireland's ancient ruins. It holds within its walls an eerie reminder of some of the most turbulent events and intriguing people from Ireland's opulent history

Ardmore Cathedral
CO. WATERFORD

Standing on a hill just above the town of Ardmore, this monastic site was founded by St Declan in the fifth century. The buildings that remain there today, however, date from the twelfth century, after the restoration of church power took place.

The cathedral itself has suffered from time and the elements, and stands pretty much a ruin, although the Romanesque carvings on the outer walls are still quite magnificent. They depict biblical scenes, including the Adoration of the Magi and a fine carving of the Archangel Michael weighing the souls on Judgement Day.

In stark contrast to the ruins of the cathedral, the round tower is one of the most well-preserved in Ireland. It stands to a height of 30 metres. One of the most interesting features of this tower is the door, which is attached to the wall almost four metres above the ground. This would have provided increased protection for those hiding inside from attackers – who ranged from Viking warriors, to people who simply resented the affluence and prosperity of the monasteries at the time.

Kilkenny Castle
CO. KILKENNY

Kilkenny is one of Ireland's most beautiful and historic towns. It is dominated by the castle, which was built in 1172 by the first Norman conqueror of Ireland, Richard de Clare (Strongbow). Although the castle retains its medieval structure, it has undergone many alterations over the centuries. William the Marshall who took over the castle on the death of Strongbow, transformed it into a stone fortress, and, much later, the Victorian owners imposed Gothic-Revival changes, which have had the most lasting impact on the castle's style.

In 1391, the Butler dynasty, later the Earls of Ormonde, adopted Kilkenny Castle, and their descendants occupied it right up until 1935. A large part of their continued favour in Ireland and the longevity of their reign in Kilkenny was due to their political astuteness. Throughout the centuries, the constant changes in religious following dictated by the regime in England, were matched accordingly by the Butlers, who had both Protestant and Catholic branches. In 1967, the Marquis of Ormonde donated the castle to the Irish nation, and now this distinguished building is open for all to admire.

Round Towers at Clonmacnoise
CO. OFFALY

The remains of two Round Towers still grace the awesome monastic settlement at Clonmacnoise, one of which can be seen here through a window of the ancient building. These two towers were named after the leaders who initiated their construction, and they both date from the early twelfth century.

The larger of the two, O'Rourke's Tower, was damaged by lightening in 1135, only a short time after it was completed, but it is believed that the monks continued to use it – unrepaired – as a place of refuge in times of attack for over 400 years. The conical roof that would once have crowned the tower is now missing, but one can still see the eight slit windows at the top that would have been used as lookout points over the surrounding countryside to warn of oncoming danger. MacCarthy's Tower is in better repair than its neighbour, although smaller. This particular round tower is unusual in that its entrance, generally designed at a strategic level a way up the tower itself, is actually at ground level here.

The Grianán of Aileach
CO. DONEGAL

The Grianán of Aileach ('House of the Sun') is one of Donegal's most remarkable and fascinating monuments. This ancient circular stone fort has a long and varied history: it is believed to have been built in the fifth century as a pagan temple, although this is a speculative date. Hundreds of years later it was taken over by the Christians. The walls of the Grianán are incredibly thick, and are marked by two passages that start at either side of the entrance, and run inside the walls halfway round the fort. This magnificent fortification was, at one time, home to the Kings of Ulster of the O'Neill dynasty, but despite the strong defences, it was partially destroyed by the King of Munster and his armies in the twelfth century. Restored in the late nineteenth century, this is now one of the most intriguing landmarks in Ireland.

Standing at the peak of a 240-metre mountain, the views from the ramparts of the Grianán of Aileach are truly awe-inspiring. From this vantage point, the beauty of the Loughs Swilly and Foyle can be seen at their very best, and all around, the lush green countryside of Ireland abounds in all its glory.

Carved Figures at White Island
CO. FERMANAGH

These curious figures are carved into one of the walls of the ruined church on White Island, which lies in the north-east of Lough Erne. The church itself dates from the twelfth century, but it is clear these figures come from a much earlier period. It is possible that they were originally part of a monastery that stood on this site.

Although there are many statues and relics of pre-Christian times throughout Ireland, no other group provides such a paradox. It is widely believed that half these figures are pagan and half Christian. They are a combination of the characteristic grotesque pagan style and that of the sombre early Christian figures. The name given to statues such as these is *sheela na gigs*, and both archeologists and anthropologists have struggled for years now to interpret the meaning of these fascinating statues.

These are not the only statues to have mysterious meanings and origins in this area, though. Not far away from White Island, on Boa Island in the north of Lough Erne, there stand two double-faced figures. Although they are clearly pagan in style, they lie conspicuously in the middle of a deserted Christian cemetery. How these statues came to be here, what their purposes were and what rituals were associated with them is another fascinating mystery.

Donegal Castle
CO. DONEGAL

Standing by the banks of the River Eske, Donegal Castle was home to the famous O'Donnell family from 1474. The family lost the house to the English in 1601 after the Battle of Kinsale, in which O'Donnell and his army were badly defeated. Before they marched from the castle, however, the patriotic O'Donnell decided to destroy his own home, and set fire to the building. This was a tactical decision to prevent the English from seizing the castle and using it as a fortress for their own ends to attack the Irish.

Sadly, this is exactly what happened: Basil Brooke was granted the castle in 1611. Brooke extended the manor house into a fortified tower, which can still be seen today. The castle was kept in the Brooke family for several generations before falling into a state of ruin in the eighteenth century. Donegal was eventually handed over to the Office of the Public Works in 1898. Much work has been done on the castle in recent years, and it now almost restored to its former splendour, presiding majestically once again over the town of Donegal.

Enniskillen Castle
CO. FERMANAGH

Lying proudly on the shores of the River Erne, Enniskillen Castle was originally designed and built in the fifteenth century by the chieftains in this part of Northern Ireland. After two centuries of use, it was falling into disrepair, and in the seventeenth century was taken over by William Cole, who repaired, rebuilt and extended the castle.

One of the finest additions Cole made to Enniskillen Castle was the Watergate: a magnificent tower, added to the outer walls of the castle. The twin turrets of Watergate enhance the beauty of the building, and transform the castle from a standard fifteenth-century structure into a place that is reminiscent of tales of old: of chivalry and honour, knights and ladies. Enniskillen now reflects something of Ireland's great love of magic and fairy tale.

The impressive three-storey castle keep was once a medieval castle itself, and later became a military barracks. Today the keep houses an interesting exhibition, and other parts of the castle are home to many fascinating objects that tell of ancient times and traditions.

Monastery at Clonmacnoise
CO. OFFALY

The remains of the monastic settlement at Clonmacnoise must be among the most extraordinary and impressive of the many relics of Ireland's past. Standing on a tranquil and remote hill by the banks of the River Shannon, this isolated site bears the ruins not only of the sixth-century monastery, but also of a cathedral, churches, a castle, and two round towers. Scattered eerily around the site are also numerous grave slabs, standing stones and various high crosses.

Founded in AD 548 by St Ciaran, the settlement was originally built on the crossroads of many routes through Ireland, and as such became a thriving community of religion and scholarship. In less peaceful times, it was plundered by the Vikings and the Normans, and eventually fell to the English in 1552. It has become the burial place of kings, and its silent, decaying stones tell of centuries of change. Pilgrims still make their way to Clonmacnoise every year on 9 September, to honour the saint who founded the settlement, St Ciaran. The attraction this site holds to visitors all year round is a testimony to the aura of peace and reverence that hangs over this beautiful spot even today.

Dundrum Castle
CO. DOWN

The village of Dundrum takes its name from *Dun Droma*, meaning 'Fort of the Ridge', and is a beautiful place surrounded by acres of trees, and with a plethora of fascinating wildlife, including seals. Surveying the town, from the vantage point of a small hill just to the north-west, stand the ruins of a Norman castle.

The origins of this castle lie with John de Courcy, an English knight who came to Ireland with a large army on the orders of Henry II of England, with the intention of capturing Ulster. Having chosen a strategic site on a rocky promontory, he began Dundrum in 1177. It was just one of a chain of forts lining the coast, and it is now recognisable as one of the first of the new Norman designs in stone building. The fort was built in keeping with this new style, which included a large keep accessed by a spiral stone staircase, and a ditch cut into the rock as a reinforced defence measure. Also on the site is evidence of two enclosed courtyards and a house, dating from the seventeenth century.

O'Brien's Castle
CO. GALWAY

O'Brien's Castle stands on the isle of Inisheer, one of the three Aran islands that lie just off the coast of Galway. The O'Briens of Munster were a strong tribe and fought for supremacy of the Aran islands, against the O'Flahertys of Connacht for many years in medieval times. The first in this line was Turlough O'Brien, and the family became the earls of Tomond, a title which they held, on and off, right up until 1847.

The castle stands on a rocky limestone hill – the only hill on the island – and its silhouette can be seen looming against the Atlantic skyline as the island is approached. It was built in the fourteenth century on the site of, and from the stones of,

an ancient fort called Dun Formna, which had stood on the island since prehistoric times. O'Brien's Castle itself has now fallen into ruin, destroyed by Cromwell's troops in 1652 and, unrepaired since that time, it is just one of the many forts and towers built by this clan that lie as relics all over Ireland in testimony to their strength.

Dunluce Castle
CO. ANTRIM

Dating from the thirteenth century, Dunluce Castle was once the main fortress of the MacDonnell chiefs, and was frequently besieged by their many enemies. The main event in its history dates from the Spanish Armada, when Philip II of Spain sent 141 ships out from Lisbon to destroy the English fleet and win the fight against Protestantism. By the time the ships reached Ireland, however, the force of the English fleet, and strong gales that blew across from Scotland had wreaked havoc on the Armada. The ships that had not sunk were overloaded with rescued sailors from other ships, and could not complete their mission. When the *Girona* sunk just off the coast near Dunluce it took with her all but nine of her 1300 men. MacDonnell, a fiercely anti-English Irishman, took in the survivors – and a large amount of the booty they had been carrying.

The ruins of the castle stand in eerie isolation, dangerously close to the edge of a steep crag (its precarious position was emphasised in 1639, when a storm actually blew the castle kitchens into the sea). If there are ghosts still in Ireland, they must surely walk the cobbled courtyards of Dunluce.

LOUGHS & MOUNTAINS

The loughs and mountains are the most breathtaking elements of the Irish landscape. The peaks of the vivid blue and grey mountains disappear into the wild clouds, and the loughs shimmer magnificently in the lowlands.

The Lakes of Killarney
CO. KERRY

The Killarney Lakes, and the surrounding areas are not surprisingly some of the most popular places to visit in Ireland. The scenery in this part of Co. Kerry is nothing short of spectacular. The lakes themselves provide an atmosphere of peace and tranquillity, set in a landscape that is scattered with the silent ruins of ancient castles and abbeys, rich woodland and the magnificent mountain peaks of the Macgillcuddys, the highest mountain range in Ireland.

The Upper Lake is the smallest of the three, and it flows down through the Long Range River, which connects the lakes in a place romantically called the Meeting of the Waters. Here the other two lakes, Muckcross and Lough Leane, connect with Upper Lake in a beautiful and impressive merger. The rapids here at the Meeting of the Waters are particularly spectacular.

The Lakes of Killarney have proved to be the inspiration of many writers, for their outstanding beauty and calm, and their ever-changing shifts of light and colour as they catch the reflections of the mountains or the clouds.

Lough Corrib
CO. GALWAY

This picturesque, traditional thatched cottage lies on the banks of Lough Corrib, the largest lake in the Republic of Ireland. Lough Corrib takes its name from the sea god Oirbsiu Mac Alloid (the lake used to be named Loch Oirbsen), known as Manannan Mac Lir. Legend has it that in ancient times a great battle took place on the western shores between Manannan Mac Lir and Uillin, in which Manannan Mac Lir was slain by his opponent. The area in which this battle is believed to have taken place is known as Magh-Uillin.

As well as the legends associated with Lough Corrib, it also has many historical associations – some of which are still evident today. On the island of Inchagoill, which lies in the middle of the Lough, can be found the remains of an ancient monastic settlement including two churches. There are in fact 365 islands like this

rising silently out of the calm waters. These are mainly small and uninhabited, and are the home to various species of wildlife and birds such as coots and swans, who nest along the banks.

Lough Allen
CO. LEITRIM

Lough Allen, with Lough Ree and Lough Derg, make up the great Shannon Lakes. Together these three form a large part of the river that runs through the heart of Ireland. As one travels down the River Shannon, the landscape changes quite significantly. Around Lough Allen, the horizon is largely covered by drumlins – the somewhat bleak, low mountains that are characteristic of this area of the country. The rocky landscape, however, does not detract from the beauty, peace and tranquillity of the lake area.

The lake is the first on the Shannon, and stretches for three miles. Its size and great depth make it the largest Lough in the area and, like many of the other freshwater sheets in Ireland, it is a haven for fishermen. Anglers are drawn by the reputation for beauty and serenity of these lakes – and most importantly the abundance of fish that are found in their waters, including pike and bream.

It is not only anglers that are attracted by the beauty of this lake. Living and nesting along the shores of Lough Allen are many forms of water birds and other wildlife. Swans are a common sight on these lakes, and are not disturbed by the occasional interruptions from those peacefully fishing in the waters of their home.

Fishing on Lough Corrib
CO. GALWAY

Stretching approximately 35 miles from Galway to Mam, Lough Corrib is one of the largest areas of freshwater in Ireland. Although the lake lies close to the bustling town of Galway, and other villages and towns dot the landscape surrounding the lake, it remains a peaceful area, and as such it is also one of the most popular places for fishermen.

A plethora of fish live in the lake including trout, salmon and pike, and all year round the shores of Corrib are scattered with anglers, who come from all over the country to fish in the lake. But it is not only the line fisherman who come here. The size of the Lough, and the rich harvest of fresh fish it yields means that small fishing boats with nets like this one are also seen up and down the lake.

This is one of the three main great fishing lakes in Ireland, the others being Lough Mask and Lough Carra. Together they form a chain of water that is both beautiful and productive.

Lough Eske
CO. DONEGAL

Lough Eske means 'Lake of the Fish'. Although the Irish lakes are generally noted for their abundance and diverse range of fish, Lough Eske has been superseded in popularity by places such as Lough Corrib and Lough Mask. Eske remains famous, however, for its rare fish called a charr. This is a member of the salmon family, and is distinctively marked by pink spots on a black body. The charr was named after the Third Earl of Enniskillen who provided the first specimen of this type in the 1860s. Other than the charr, few fish grace the placid waters of Lough Eske.

While fish-life may be scarce, however, visitors to the Lough can enjoy searching for the lake's other renowned inhabitant – the freshwater

oyster, which thrives in the sand on the banks of the Lough. Some of these are even reputed to contain pearls, but few will ever find them. Set against the picture-postcard magnificence of the Blue Stack Mountains, this is a beautiful place simply to enjoy the peace and solitude.

Slievemore Mountain
CO. MAYO

Over these pleasant whitewashed cottages looms the formidable Slievemore Mountain. From the top of Slievemore, one can survey the whole of Achill – the wild and rugged island from which it rises majestically in the northern regions. The mountain stands at a height of 671 metres above sea level, and is a magnificent landmark, dominating the island and overshadowing much of the landscape with its dark and mysterious influence.

Adding to the atmosphere of wilderness on Achill Island, the deserted village of Slievemore lies at the foot of the mountain, tucked protectively away in the shadows. The village is one of the most fascinating and eerie sites on the island. This settlement was deserted during the Great Famine, and has been uninhabited since then. There are approximately 75 buildings still standing on the site, in two groups: Tuar in the west of the village and Tuar Riabhach to the east. This was once a small but thriving agricultural area, and the remnants of the old practices can still be seen in the field systems. Often the animals would have been moved according to the season from the lowland into the summer pastures, which were in the lower regions of the Slievemore Mountain.

Upper Lake at Glendalough
CO. WICKLOW

Through intricate motions ran
Stream and gliding sun
And all my heart seemed gay

W. B. Yeats

Yeats's poem 'Stream and Sun at Glendalough', goes some way to describing the peace and contentment felt by visitors to this radiant area of Co. Wicklow. Literally meaning 'Glen of the Two Lakes', Glendalough is a placid but spectacularly beautiful place. The landscape in which the lakes are set is dominated by tree-covered hills, and the ruins of the ancient monastic site founded by St Kevin. The Lower Lake and the Upper Lake are equally impressive, and there are many walks through these hills, which offer dazzling views of the water, glinting serenely in the sunlight.

Like so many of Ireland's Loughs, these have an atmosphere of stillness and reverence, broken only occasionally by the flurry of a waterfall where a stream or river meets the Lough. Not far away lie many remarkable sights, including Baltinglass Abbey and Powerscourt – an impressive Palladian mansion with extensive grounds – that complement the lush countryside in which they are set.

The Twelve Bens
CO. GALWAY

Mountains in Ireland are unlike any found elsewhere in Europe. They encompass a diverse range of formations and shapes. From high, grassy hills, to bleak rocky crags, Ireland is a mountain-climber's paradise, with climbs to suit the most amateur and the most expert.

The Twelve Bens are perhaps the most famous of all the mountain ranges in Ireland because of their superb walks and climbs, and their shimmering beauty. They tower above Galway, and from the top afford views over miles of lush countryside and picturesque villages. They are not high compared to many of the famous European mountain ranges – the highest in the mass of peaks only reaches 730 metres – but they hold a mysterious appeal that warns of danger yet invites one to penetrate their mists.

The Twelve Bens are made up from groups of rocky outcrops formed from exposed white quartzite, and some of the more popular

walks along the mountains feel as though they are cut through the very heart of the rock. From some of these paths, the views across Connemara below are magnificent, and many little villages shelter in the silent protection of the Twelve Bens.

Muckish Mountain
CO. DONEGAL

The high plateau rising proudly in the background of these cottages in Donegal is known as Muckish Mountain, and stands at 668 metres high. It forms part of the Derryveagh Mountain range, which runs through the north-west of the country.

Muckish is one of the best known peaks in this range – the other popular mountain here is Errigal – mainly known for its walks and climbs. The mountain itself is made up of three main sections that give different but equally challenging climbs: MacSwaynes Buttress, Balors Buttress and Hogs Back Buttress. Travel into the crags of Muckish often begins at the quaint little village of Falcarragh, a Gaelic-speaking community nestling at the foot of the mountain. From here, the road takes travellers through the Muckish Gap and up the mountainside. The views such routes offer are truly spectacular, and from the top the horizon spreads out as far as Malin Head over a rich patchwork of Irish fields, lakes and hills, and particularly the surrounding area of beautiful Donegal.

Lough Fee
CO. GALWAY

The area around Lough Fee offers some of the most spectacular scenery anywhere in Ireland. The coastal road is dominated by beautiful sandy beaches, and not far away lies the famous Killary harbour. This is reputed to be the only fjord in Ireland, and is a long inlet that runs the length of approximately ten miles through the mountains. It is famed for being one of the safest anchorages in the world – the entire British fleet anchored here at one point during World War I.

Lough Fee itself lies by the small town of Salruck, which has marvellous views over the Killary Bays. The scenery around the Lough is dominated by the dark and daunting Mweelrea Mountains, rising sharply from its shores. Like most of the other Irish lakes, Lough Fee has a good reputation for fishing, and although not the most popular, is still a paradise for anglers. Oscar Wilde and his brother Willie grew up in this area and used to fish in Lough Fee when they were children.

Ben Bulben
CO. SLIGO

Myths and legends about Ben Bulben abound in Irish literature and oral tradition. One of the most popular is the 'Death of Diarmuid in the Boar Hunt'. The story goes that the infamous giant Finn MacCool was hunting a wild boar that had killed a number of his men on the mountain. Diarmuid, hearing his struggles, came to help, and a fight ensued in which Diarmuid showed his great strength and courage. He killed the boar in the same instant that it dealt him a fatal blow with one of its tusks. Finn MacCool, who had the power to save him through the healing waters of a nearby spring, refused to help, humiliated that the younger man had succeeded where he had failed. Diarmuid died on the slopes of Ben Bulben, and today there is a place on the mountain named the Cave of Diarmuid.

Today, Ben Bulben is best known for its association with the poet W. B. Yeats, and for its dramatic situation looming out of the Sligo plain. Its eerie aspect, and the plethora of legends associated with it, give the mountain a mysterious and fascinating appeal.

Lough Mask
CO. MAYO

The Loughs are as familiar a part of the Irish landscape as the rolling clouds and lush hills, and they contribute to the rich and fertile feel of the country. They are inhabited by all manner of birds, wildlife and plants and vary from the beautiful and tranquil to the wild and relatively undisturbed.

Lough Mask lies in Co. Mayo, the third largest county in Ireland. It is smaller and less popular than its near neighbour Lough Corrib, but has an unusual beauty and serenity. During the Great Famine, a canal was built connecting these two Loughs, but the limestone bed of the lakes proved too porous, and the experiment failed. Today, all that is left of this project are the bridges and locks along the canal between Corrib and Mask.

Lough Mask covers over 20,000 acres and is more than ten miles long. Its abundance of fish such as ferox trout, pike and eels makes it a haven for the angler. Bordered on one shore by the impressive Partry Mountains, and on the other by the picturesque village of Cong, the Lough is an enchantingly beautiful and tranquil place.

Mountains in Killarney
CO. KERRY

The highest peaks in Ireland lie in the range of mountains known as Macgillcuddy's Reeks; a semi-circle of mountains which dominate the horizon to the south and west of Killarney. The highest mountain in Ireland, Carrantuahill reaches to over 1000 metres, but is often obscured from view by other peaks, such as the Mangerton, when seen from the lowlands of this captivating area. The views from the top of both, however, are unsurpassed.

The foothills of the Reeks are covered in rich woodland that has remained untouched by the demand for timber. Further up the mountains, the trees become more sparse, and blankets of heather cover whole areas of the slopes. The walks through these mountains offer magnificent views down across the sights of Killarney, including the National Park and the famous three lakes. Other routes can take a traveller through what seems like the very core of the hills, giving a feeling of isolation in one of the most wild and remote places in the country.

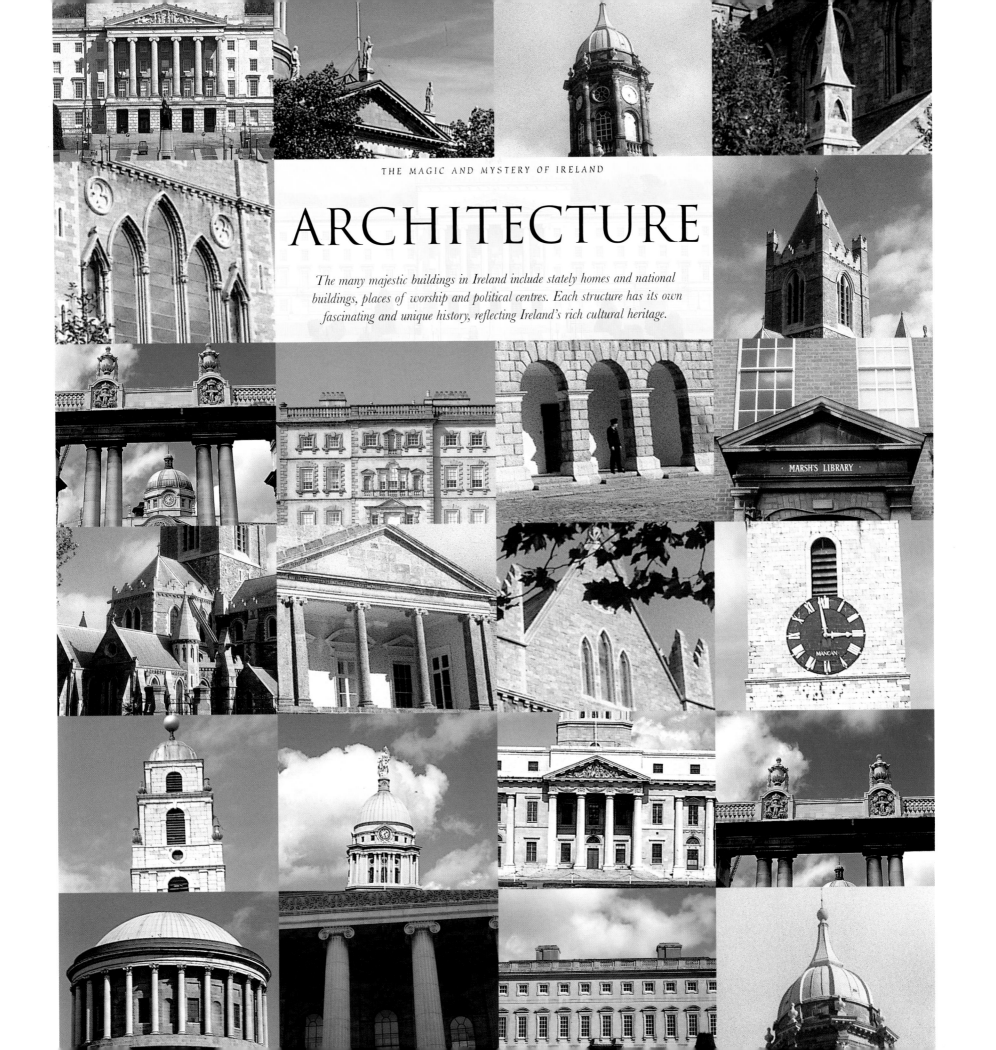

ARCHITECTURE

The many majestic buildings in Ireland include stately homes and national buildings, places of worship and political centres. Each structure has its own fascinating and unique history, reflecting Ireland's rich cultural heritage.

The Four Courts
CO. DUBLIN

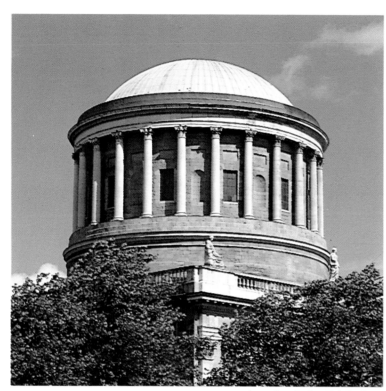

Designed by James Gandon, the same architect as the nearby Custom House in Dublin, the Four Courts stand gracefully on the banks of the River Liffey, which flows through the heart of the city. The courts are made up of a magnificent six-columned Corinthian portico, flanked by the two wings that house the Four Courts themselves: Common Pleas, Chancery, Exchequer and the King's Bench. Decorated with marvellous carved figures including those of Justice and Mercy, and topped by an impressive lantern dome, the Four Courts is an awe-inspiring building.

The original structure was erected on the site of a medieval abbey, and was started in 1786. Completed in 1802, it became the central home of the Irish Justice System. This reign came to an end abruptly in 1922, at the outbreak of the Irish Civil War when the building was taken by the anti-treaty faction, who were only driven out after a fierce battle, when government forces bombarded the courts. The resulting explosion destroyed much of the structure, and perhaps more importantly the Public Record Office nearby, which contained thousands of irreplaceable documents.

Restoration of the courts took over ten years to complete but they were carefully rebuilt according to Gandon's original designs, so the building that stands there today still revels in the magnificence that surrounded it before the revolution took place.

Castletown House
CO. KILDARE

One of the most beautiful country houses in Ireland, Castletown is a reflection of luxury and opulence. The Palladian style that it introduced from Europe began a revolution in Irish architecture.

The building was begun in 1722 for William Conolly, the son of a Donegal innkeeper, who had worked his way up to become one of the richest men in Ireland. He was also extremely influential in political circles after being elected Speaker of the Irish House of Commons. Originally the design for the house was planned by the Italian architect Alessandro Galilei who was known for his work on the Lateran Basilica in Rome. Later on, supervision for Castletown was taken over by the young Edward Lovett Pearce, who had studied under Galilei.

The impressive exterior of Castletown is dominated by the central block; classical Italian Renaissance in influence, and remarkable for its silvery limestone which has endured the elements and remains free of the stains of age. The pavilions were erected from a different, golden-brown limestone and provide a graceful contrast to the central block.

Marsh's Library
CO. DUBLIN

Situated next to St Patrick's Cathedral in the heart of Dublin, this public library was designed and built in 1701 for Archbishop Narcissus Marsh, the Dean of St Patrick's. This intriguing figure had a passion for books, particularly those on the subjects of science and mathematics. There are 25,000 volumes housed in Marsh's Library dating from the sixteenth, seventeenth and early eighteenth centuries. Included in these volumes is a remarkable copy of the *History of the Great Rebellion* that once belonged to the writer and satirist Jonathan Swift. This volume is marked with Swift's own comments (mostly derogatory!) on the Scottish.

Much of the interior of the library remains exactly as it was in Marsh's day: the bookcases are made from fine dark oak and are characterised by the sign of a mitre and beautiful gold-leaf lettering. The other fascinating parts of the library are the three wired alcoves, nicknamed the 'cages' that stand in the rear of the building. Visitors wishing to read especially valuable books were, quite literally, locked in the cages.

When he died in 1713, Archbishop Marsh bequeathed all his books to the library, and other patrons have done the same on occasion since then, so the library now carries a wealth of fascinating information on all subjects, as well as being a place of great historic interest in its own right.

The General Post Office
CO. DUBLIN

Dominating the corners of Henry and O'Connell Streets in Dublin's thriving city centre is the General Post Office. Like much of the architecture in this part of Ireland, it has a fascinating history of destruction tempered by loving restoration. It was built in 1818 by the architect Francis Johnson. Johnson's influences were largely neo-classical, and the original front façade of the building, which still remains, was built according to this style.

The General Post Office was besieged during the Easter Rising in 1916. It was taken on Easter Monday, and on the steps of the building, in what was to become a great moment in Irish history, Patrick Pearse read aloud the Proclamation of the Irish Republic. The British forces eventually ejected them from the building, but the shells that they used caused extensive damage. Like the Four Courts, it was rebuilt according to the original designs, and reopened to resume business in 1929.

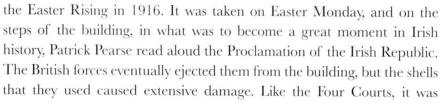

A sculpture fashioned from bronze stands in the entrance hall to the General Post Office, and depicts the dying mythical warrior knight Cuchulainn. This is dedicated to those who lost their lives in the Civil War. Its fascinating history makes this building a thought-provoking monument in the city.

The Abbey Theatre
CO. DUBLIN

In 1898, in keeping with the cultural renaissance that was sweeping the country, the poet W. B. Yeats, Lady Gregory – an aristocrat with a passion for writing and literature – and Edward Martyn, founded the Irish Literary Theatre Society. Prior to this, Ireland had no national theatre of its own, and had to rely on travelling companies, mostly from England, with English plays, to provide theatrical entertainment.

The Abbey Theatre opened its doors on a December night in 1904, and since that time, it has been committed to showing the best in Irish plays and dramas: performing established playwrights and encouraging aspiring dramatists alike. The main theatre upstairs houses the mainstream productions, and the smaller Peacock Theatre below is home to the more experimental works by amateurs.

Practically since the day it opened, the Abbey Theatre has incited controversy over the plays it has housed. There were riots during a performance of John Millington Synge's *A Playboy of the Western World*, and this was not the first or last time the easily aroused passions of the Irish were released. This only adds, however, to the interest of the theatre, which continues to honour its promise to encourage the works of all manner of Irish writers.

St Patrick's Cathedral
CO. DUBLIN

A church has stood on this land since the fifth century. In its earliest days it was a simple wooden chapel, which was replaced by the Normans in 1191. Later, in the thirteenth century it was rebuilt in the form we see it today. It is believed that St Patrick baptised converts here at a well, which was unearthed at the beginning of the twentieth century. Like much of the architecture throughout Ireland, St Patrick's Cathedral has suffered over the centuries from war and neglect. It was restored properly in the late 1800s by Sir Benjamin Guinness, a member of one of Ireland's most illustrious families.

Perhaps the most striking element of this cathedral is the massive tower which stands to the west: this was restored after a fire in 1370 by Archbishop Minot. Now known as Minot's Tower, it houses the cathedral bells, which have the loudest peal of any bells in the country. The impressive spire that reaches to 31 metres in height was added in 1749.

In keeping with Ireland's great literary heritage, the writer Jonathan Swift is buried here in the cathedral, and 'Swift's Corner' in the north transept bears many relics of the great satirist's life and work.

The Bells of Shandon
CO. CORK

With deep affection and recollection
I often think of those Shandon Bells
Whose sound so wild would, in the days of childhood
Fling around my cradle their
    magic spells
                         Father Prout

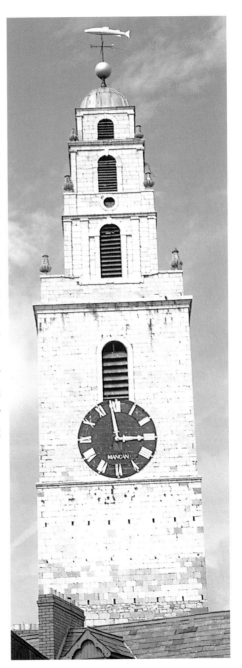

Lying at the heart of Cork city, the bell tower attached to St Anne's Church is one of the most striking landmarks in this area, and is one of Cork's most famous attractions. The tower is an unusual structure, made up of both limestone and sandstone, which makes two of the sides white and two red. On all four sides is a clock face which, until the 1980s was known by the locals as the 'four-faced liar' due to the fact that each of the clock faces told a slightly different time.

Erected in 1772, on the site of a previous church that had been destroyed in 1660, the tower is built in stages, each one smaller than the one below, and eventually pinnacled with a magnificent dome that is topped by the most distinctive of weathervanes, in the shape of a golden salmon.

The eight bells that live in the tower have received much of their widespread fame through the poem by Francis Mahony, who penned his tribute to them 'The Bells of Shandon', under the name of Father Prout. Today, they still ring out across the city of Cork in a magnificent ensemble.

Dublin Castle
CO. DUBLIN

The original building that stood on the site of Dublin Castle was a Viking stronghold, built between 1208 and 1220. Little of this now remains, except for the Record Tower that stands in the Lower Castle Yard, which has been much modified since its original erection. Recent excavations uncovered some of the ancient Danish fortress, and are now on show here. The original boundaries of the castle are still roughly maintained in the Upper Castle Yard. It was rebuilt after a fire wreaked havoc on the building in 1684.

The interior of the castle is much more spectacular than its external appearance seems to imply, and the building is full of fascinating rooms

and halls which hold relics of times past. The main part of the castle, on the upper floors has been converted into a suite of luxury apartments that are now used for national functions. One of the most magnificent rooms is the Throne Room. This was last used officially when George V of England visited Ireland, and the throne itself is conjectured to have been presented to the castle by William of Orange after his success on the battlefields of the Boyne.

The Custom House
CO. DUBLIN

Standing majestically on the banks of the River Liffey, the Custom House is a magnificent tribute to its designer James Gandon. Gandon was an English architect, who took his influences from Europe, and he went on to contribute many other fine buildings to the city of Dublin.

Building started on the Custom House in 1781, and it took ten years to complete. Its front is a beautiful Doric portico flanked by two pavilions. There are 14 sculpted figures on the keystones, which represent the 13 main rivers of Ireland and the Atlantic Ocean. These were created by a local sculptor named Edward Smyth, who is also responsible for the statue of Commerce that surveys the city from the peak of the 38 metre copper dome on the top of the Custom House.

In 1800 the Customs and Excise trade was moved away from Dublin to London, and this grand building was denied the purpose for which it was built after only ten years of service. It stood decaying for many years, until a fire in 1921 virtually gutted the whole place. Although restoration began in 1926, it was not fully completed until much later, and the Custom House was reopened – to be used as government offices – on its bicentenary in 1991.

Florence Court
CO. FERMANAGH

Exactly who designed Florence Court is unknown, and the precise date of its conception and origins are equally ambiguous. The original building, however, is believed to have been begun around 1718 for the Cole family. The house that still stands today was constructed later than this though, probably during the 1750s by John Cole. The Court was named after his wife Florence Wray. Like many of the other stately homes in Ireland – Powerscourt and Castletown amongst them – Florence Court is Palladian in style, a splendid, luxurious building set amongst acres of wilderness and carefully sculptured gardens.

The front façade of the three-storey house, with its gold-and-silver colouring, is beautifully ornate with a baroque feel to it, and has Rococco plasterwork, but the remaining sides of the house are plain in comparison, a characteristic of houses in Ireland dating from the eighteenth century. Sadly, much of the house was destroyed by fire in the 1950s, but it has been carefully restored and remains one of Northern Ireland's most magical houses.

Christ Church Cathedral
CO. DUBLIN

In 1038, the Vikings built a wooden church on the site of what is now Christ Church Cathedral. The building that stands there today was commissioned in 1172 by Laurence O'Toole – who later became St Laurence – and the infamous Norman knight Richard de Clare, known as Strongbow. His remains are interred in the cathedral and the heart of St Laurence is also contained here in a metal casket. With the English religious reforms in the 1530s, the cathedral was adopted by the Protestant Church of Ireland.

Over the centuries since it was first constructed, Christ Church has undergone many restorations, particularly in the nineteenth century, when the architect George Street, took the derelict building and made new designs for it in the Gothic style. These ideas were adopted and funded by Henry Roe to the tune of the present day equivalent of over 20 million pounds. During the many restorations that the building has seen, not all the monuments and other objects of interest were disposed of, and many now reside in the crypt of the present building.

The Government Buildings
CO. DUBLIN

In Upper Merrion Street in Dublin lie the Government Buildings of the Republic of Ireland, where the offices of the Prime Minister (*Taoiseach*) and other members of Parliament are housed. Standing gracefully next to the Natural History Museum, this splendid building was restored in the early 1990s.

Over two centuries ago, the original Irish Houses of Parliament were erected on one side of College Green. The architect on these buildings was Edward Lovett Pearce, but the structure was sadly not completed until after his death in 1739. The eastern facade of the building was added by the architect James Gandon in 1785. The parliament building did not serve the purpose for which it was constructed for very long: in 1800, when the Act of Union came into effect, the government was moved to London, and took much of the Irish aristocracy and affluence with it. The building was later bought by the Bank of Ireland and underwent some remodelling to adapt it for its new purpose, but significant amounts of the interior remain as they were in its heyday, including the fabulous House of Lords, which is now open to visitors. The splendour of the government buildings on Upper Merrion Street can also be enjoyed by visiors one day a week.

Stormont
CO. ANTRIM

Lying about four miles to the east of Belfast, Stormont is a large, elegant building, designed along similar lines to Buckingham Palace, set at the end of a long straight avenue amid acres of lush park land. It was built between 1928 and 1932, and the whole project cost over one million pounds – funded by the British government. This grand and stately building was designed in the Palladian style, and was made from Portland stone and granite from Mourne in Co. Down, rather than the traditional limestone blocks that characterise much other architecture in both Northern and Southern Ireland – mainly because it was available locally and cheaply.

Stormont was originally created to house the Northern Ireland Parliament – a suitable grandiose building for the matters of national importance that were to be decided there. It was not to serve this purpose for long, however, and after the first Parliament closed in 1972, it has never been reopened for parliamentary use again. Since this time, it has become the centre of the government administration, housing only offices.

THE MAGIC AND MYSTERY OF IRELAND

LANDSCAPES

In no other country are there such diverse and beautiful landscapes. From the harsh rocks and formidable cliffs that border the wild Atlantic, to the bright hills and tame woodland of inland counties, Ireland is a land of unsurpassed beauty.

Drumcliff Cemetery,
CO. SLIGO

The poet W. B. Yeats – one of the best known of all Ireland's literary figures – is buried here at Drumcliff cemetery, in the romantic shadow of the great Ben Bulben mountain, in Co. Sligo, North-West Ireland.

Yeats's mother was the daughter of a shipping merchant in Sligo, and although Yeats grew up in London, many of his holidays were spent with his mother's family. He grew to love Ireland passionately, and eventually returned there to pursue his writing: this affection for the country of his birth is mirrored in much of his poetry. After his return to Ireland, Yeats became a supporter of the campaign for Irish nationalism. He fervently believed in a national literature that would eventually unite the disparate factions of the nation. This romantic ideal gradually faded, however, and his later poems reflect his disillusion in this 'blind, bitter land'.

Yeats always considered Sligo to be his home, and requested that he be buried here. His gravestone in the churchyard at Drumcliff bears the epitaph that he wrote himself: 'Cast a cold eye, On life, on death. Horseman, pass by!'.

Sunset in Donegal
CO. DONEGAL

This photograph is a perfect representation of the county of Donegal: a place of extreme beauty and serenity. The population of this part of Ireland is concentrated mainly on the rugged coastline in the small inlets that indent it, and, as such, the areas further inland are great open spaces of warm countryside, dotted with cool, clear sheets of fresh water and an abundance of wildlife.

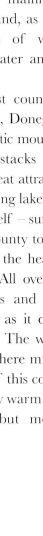

The northernmost county in the Republic of Ireland, Donegal is dominated by the dramatic mountain ranges of the Bluestacks and Derryveagh. Its other great attraction is its numerous, captivating lakes and rivers. Donegal town itself – surprisingly not actually the county town – lies on Donegal Bay at the head of the lovely River Eske. All over the county, the small pools and lakes reflect the evening sun as it disappears over the horizon. The warm, silent evening captured here mirrors the temperate climate of this county, which is characterised by warm clear summers, and fresh but modest winters.

Trinity College
CO. DUBLIN

This famous college in the heart of Dublin city was founded by Elizabeth I of England in 1592, with the intention of 'civilising' the Irish, and increasing Protestant power in Dublin. The college itself lifted its barriers on Catholic students in 1873, but it remained a largely Protestant institution until the 1960s. It is made up from some of the finest architecture in the city, particularly the Rubrics, a fine red-brick building which was built in 1700 – the oldest surviving part of the college.

Perhaps the most famous feature of Trinity College is the *Book of Kells* which is housed here. Presented to the college in the 1600s to save it from potential destruction by Cromwell's armies, this celebrated Celtic manuscript dates from the eighth century. It contains lavishly illuminated inscriptions of the gospels, and is the most famous of all Ireland's treasures.

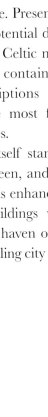

The college itself stands on the edge of College Green, and within its walls, two courtyards enhance the rich majesty of the buildings with their green lawns. It is a haven of peace in the midst of the bustling city of Dublin.

Sunset in the Aran Islands
CO. GALWAY

The landscapes of the Aran Islands are perhaps the most dramatic to be found anywhere in Ireland. Appearing like an off-cut of the wild and untamed Burren in Co. Clare, the grey rocks dominate the scenery in a formidable yet marvellous aspect. The sun setting over the islands therefore creates one of the most impressive, wild and fantastic scenes to be seen anywhere in Ireland. The light reflects off the rocks giving colour to the barren land and revealing it in its most impressive splendour.

The solitude and isolation of the islands makes them even more awesome. The pounding of the Atlantic waves below echoes off the crags and cliffs, disturbing the silence, and the wind howls across the exposed areas unbroken by any buildings or trees.

The islands, in all their austere magnificence, have inspired large numbers of writers and artists, who have visited them and been overawed by the rough landscapes, prehistoric monuments, and the ancient customs and beliefs of the islanders. The most significant of these was John Millington Synge, the famous Irish playwright who visited the island every summer and, profoundly affected by the Aran Islands, drew on the life and culture of this place as his inspiration.

Lisdoonvarna
CO. CLARE

Lying just north and inland of the wild and spectacular Cliffs of Moher, in the heart of the rocky Burren landscape, Lisdoonvarna was once a small spa town. It began to increase in popularity in the nineteenth century, when Victorian ladies and gentlemen would come to take the healing waters. These waters were rich in minerals such as iron, sulphur and iodine.

Today, however, this town is best known for its annual match-making festival. This tradition began when farmers from Co. Clare would meet here at a small festival when the harvest had been gathered and they had leisure to socialise, in the hope of acquiring a wife. This tradition has been adapted in recent years into a festival that sees people travelling from all over the world to come

and dance and sing at this essentially single celebration. Co. Clare lies at the very heart of the Irish musical tradition, and this festival is no exception: the entertainment here reflects the Irish love of their own music, and the festival itself is an enjoyable mixture of contemporary ideas and old Irish traditions.

Old Cottage
CO. DONEGAL

The picturesque remains of this old cottage lie near the town of Glenties in Donegal; it is a touching reminder of sadder times in the country when many inhabitants were forced into immigration by the severity of the Potato Famine. Today, such cottages make a graceful addition to the countryside, where they lie quietly undisturbed, surrounded by wild flowers and animals, in fields and pastures. The remoteness of this spot only adds to its beauty.

Nearby Glenties was once a successful 'Planters town', and has grown up at the beautiful point where two glens meet. Today it is a neat, well-kept little town, in keeping with Donegal's reputation for picturesque spots. Donegal comes from the Irish *Dun Na Ngall*, meaning 'Fort of the Stones' – an appropriate title for a county that is also famed for its historic associations. It is cottages such as this which make up the rich cultural heritage of which Donegal has such an abundance to offer.

Connemara
CO. GALWAY

Connemara covers the western coastal area of Galway, stretching from the banks of the grandiose Lough Corrib to the Atlantic Ocean. The area is renowned for its imposing landscapes and large parts of Connemara are characterised by hard granite. The lowlands are mainly bogs and as such, the land is not useful for agriculture, however it has some exceptional scenery surrounding it. The tall, distinguished peaks of the Maamturk Mountains, and the majestic Twelve Bens glower protectively over the area, giving it an aura of wild magnificence.

The aspect that makes Connemara so special, however, and attracts people from miles around, is the overwhelming amount of water that dominates the area. Everywhere in Connemara, one is pursued by the sound of rushing water, coming from myriad sparkling lakes, rivers and waterfalls. Glistening pools lie hidden and tranquil in the shadows of the hills, and the lowlands are split into hundreds of tiny islands, surrounded by ponds that lie winking at the changing shadows and colours of the scenery.

Achill Island
CO. MAYO

Achill comes form the Latin word *aquila* meaning 'eagle' – an appropriate name to describe the untamed nature of this island. Achill is the largest island off the west coast of the country, and is characterised by rugged coastlines, wild moors, awesome cliffs and exceptional beaches. The somewhat exposed climate has made it a haven for wind surfers and other water-sports fanatics, and climbers, who brave the dark and domineering slopes of the Slievemore Mountain which stands to the north of the island, with the just reward of a most spectacular vista from the summit.

From the mainland, the sun shining through the clouds seems to set the island afire, a dramatic scene in the middle of the ocean, the formidable clouds a fitting backdrop for one of the wildest and most beautiful spots in Ireland, particularly amongst the islands that surround the Irish coast. The views across the island are truly magnificent, and from the cliffs it is occasionally even possible to see the sharks that inhabit the water below.

Galway Bay
CO. GALWAY

Galway Bay is the most famous – and the most extensive – bay in Ireland. Set in the Atlantic Ocean just off from the city of Galway itself, it is perhaps the county's finest feature. It was the city's location here that was responsible for its commercial success, and this is probably still true today.

The people of Galway are proud of this asset, and of its history, which tells of Norman invasions, and Spanish tradesmen, who were the first to bring imports of wine across the Atlantic, and began what would grow into an enormous industry for the area. The people maintain many of the ancient customs and traditions of their heritage, including boat races round the bay. Every year a fleet of boats participates in an age-old custom of a blessing which takes place in the water and is performed by a priest. The boats leave the quayside and form a circle in the bay, they receive the blessing and pray for good weather and an abundant harvest of fish, just as fishermen have done throughout the centuries.

Spring Day
CO. CLARE

Spring is perhaps the most favourable time in which to experience Ireland. A land of luscious greenery, the colours of Ireland are at their freshest and most dazzling in the spring months, when the rains have washed everything, the rivers and lakes are clear and fresh and even the mountains rise from the ground in vibrant shades of blue, grey and purple. The wild flowers that dominate the Irish meadows and pastures are just blooming and there is an ethereal, magical quality to the landscape.

The dramatic contrast of the rocky Clare landscape and the marvellous rushing spring clouds is typically Irish. Clear blue skies can be seen over Ireland in the heat of summer and the cloud formations are famed throughout the world, for the dramatic impact they have on the passing countryside. They encourage constant shifts and changes in light and colour, making a place mysterious and forbidding one minute, then shifting to allow pale sunshine to bathe the fields and mountain peaks in warmth. Wherever you are in the country it is worth spending some time watching the breathtaking effects of the Irish skies on the land below.

The Blasket Islands
CO. KERRY

Lying off the coast of Dingle in Co. Kerry, the six islands that make up the Blaskets are the last European land mass in the Atlantic. They are characterised by their harsh and rocky landscape and their rugged beauty. Until the 1930s they were inhabited by only a handful of people, braving the harsh climate – an isolated civilisation. Today, they are some of Ireland's most famous uninhabited islands: even the tourists can only reach one of them, Great Blasket. The accessible island still bears evidence of its previous dwellers: the remains of a village lie just below the landing place, and above this are a group of derelict houses that were built for the poorer inhabitants.

There are spectacular views of the islands from the mainland, such as the one pictured here, and from the steep cliffs of Great Blasket, home

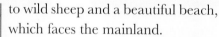

to wild sheep and a beautiful beach, which faces the mainland.

The Blasket islands are perhaps most famed for their literary heritage. Three famous Irish writers hail from these islands alone – Tomas O'Cromthain, Peig Sawyers and Maurice O'Sullivan. The islands also provided inspiration for a number of other great literary figures including W. B. Yeats.

Inisheer
CO. GALWAY

Apart from the meagre living to be earned from the land on Inisheer in the Aran Islands, the main industry is fishing, and this has been the case since the first settlers inhabited the islands in prehistoric times.

The Atlantic Ocean that crashes wildly around the islands is a haven for fishermen, yielding many types of catch, and in ancient times, fishermen would brave the dangers of this lifestyle to take their boats out. Even today, in keeping with the traditions that have remained a fundamental part of Aran life, the men take out the currach (small, locally-made boats) to try their luck in the waters. In this, as in many other ways, the islanders, continue to use the ancient methods and ways of their ancestors. This trade is made even more precarious when you consider that the ocean around these islands is home to sharks, yet fishers still take out these small, light craft to catch the immense and impressive creatures. Today, the tourist trade has supplemented the islands' economy, but fishing remains its largest industry.

Valentia Island
CO. KERRY

From Brays Head at the westernmost tip of Valentia Island, the Atlantic Ocean stretches off into the distance – an uninterrupted body of water for 1900 miles, broken finally by the shores of Newfoundland. As the most westerly point of Europe, this island became the end of the first transatlantic cable in 1858 (although permanent communication did not happen until 1866).

The island is small, and almost completely cultivated. There is none of the wild romance of much of the mainland countryside to be seen here. But Valentia has its own unique charms. Lying in the Gulf Stream, it has an unusually warm climate, and as such, an impressive display of flora and fauna thrive on the island. The most obvious of these is the fuchsia, which sprouts among the hedgerows in abundance.

For all its differences, however, Valentia still contains many aspects of typical Irish life, and music and dance are popular pastimes in the small towns dotted around the island. The social centre of this island is Knightstown, a small fishing port linked to the mainland. At one time, Valentia was a solitary mass in the ocean, but since 1972 it has been linked by bridge to the mainland at Portmagee. This has not detracted from the charms of this enchanting place or its people.

Rocky Landscape
CO. KERRY

This breathtaking vista forms part of the Dingle Peninsula – a place of diverse and marvellous natural beauty, filled with lush hills, hidden inlets and caves, and cool, clear sheets of water. The land shown here is part of the rockier scenery that characterises part of this varied landscape, and indeed, much of the Irish coastline. The rugged mountains and cliffs tower over the softer parts of the countryside and the sandy beaches and bays.

Kerry also has a wealth of ancient ruins, for those who have the will to explore the countryside. The Dingle Peninsula is one of the most ancient sites in the land, with a history of habitation spanning over 6000 years. The marks of various tribes and races stand in testimony amid the fields and rocks of Co. Kerry. From the first prehistoric peoples, through Bronze and Stone Age civilisations, through medieval races and to the locals today, the marks of ages are seen in standing stones, tombs, graves, primitive dwelling places and other stone relics all over the countryside. It is a magical place, each monument telling a story of ancient settlers, through wars and peace times until they became one race of people.

The Isle of Innisfree
CO. SLIGO

W. B. Yeats dedicated much of his poetry to his home country, often reflecting on the beauty and calm of Ireland, in contrast to the impersonal and busy surroundings in London and other European cities where he spent much of his life.

One of his most beautiful poems, 'The Lake Isle of Innisfree', reflects this passion and yearning for the solitude of the Irish countryside:

I will arise and go now, and go to Innisfree,
And a small cabin build there, of clay and
*   wattles made;*
Nine bean-rows will I have there, a hive for
*   the honeybee,*
And live alone in the bee-loud glade.

Innisfree lies to the south of Lough Gill: a pleasant, placid lake, overlooked by the ruins of a castle, and guarded now only by the water fowl that make their nests along its banks. The island is a small, romantic place, and although it is unlikely to be as remote and undisturbed now as it was when Yeats wrote his poem – possibly because of the fame his poem brought to this spell-binding place – it is still easy to see where the poet gained his inspiration, and his love of Ireland.

VIEW OF KINVARRA
CO. GALWAY

The picturesque village of Kinvarra lies on the south-east inlet of Galway Bay, and is one of the most charming places in the county, with stunning views across the water. Kinvarra is a typical Irish fishing village, it has a beautiful stone quayside, with swans and other wildfowl drifting in and out of the quay enjoying the beauty and tranquillity of the village and its surroundings. The harbour is still used by those sailing on the Galway Hookers – the traditional wooden sailing boats that were once used to carry peat, livestock and beer.

Close by, on the shore of Galway Bay, is Dunguaire Castle. This was once the home of King Guaire, who was renowned for his generosity, throwing banquets and lavish entertainments, although the castle that stands there today dates from the later period of the sixteenth century. At the castle today, banquets are still held in medieval style, Irish music is played and poetry read. Seen here silhouetted against the evening skyline is the familiar sight of a Celtic high cross.

Dingle
CO. KERRY

Apart from settlements on the islands that are scattered in the Atlantic Ocean off the coasts of Ireland, Dingle is the most western town in Europe. It is picturesquely bordered on one side by the sea and on the other by a mass of beautiful, rolling hills, that reflect the changing lights of the sky at different times of day, and provide a magnificent vista of countryside.

Dingle was once an isolated village, set apart from the other towns in Kerry, and confining itself to the local Gaelic dialect. Today, it has grown into an attractive and bustling fishing port. Part of its success is due

to the smuggling industry, which centred itself around the bay in days of yesteryear. It was also briefly the location for self-minted coinage. Although both these practices have long since been suppressed, the town continues to prosper as the main point on the Dingle Peninsula, and is a good starting point for exploring the fascinating and resplendent country-side that borders the area on all sides.

The Minaun Cliffs
CO. MAYO

The Minaun Cliffs are situated on the southern coast of Achill Island off the shores of Co. Mayo. The island covers 55 miles and is the largest island off the Irish coast. It is a beautiful and unspoilt region of the country, with landscapes of heather-covered moorland and blue mountains rising high above the sea.

The cliffs lie at the end of the Trawmroe Beach – a beautiful stretch of sand that extends for over two miles along the coastline. From the cliffs' edge is a sheer drop nearly 250 metres into the crashing Atlantic below. The cliffs run from Keel, a small village in the south-west of the island to Doeega, and the almighty views that can be seen from the land's edge are both dramatic and terrifying. These are the highest cliffs in the British Isles; from their top, it is possible to gaze out into the ocean and spot the sharks that infest the waters around the rocks below. Men still brave the waters in their currachs to catch the sharks and other fish, of which there are over 70 species in this area.

The Sperrins
CO. TYRONE

Lying to the south of Londonderry in Northern Ireland, the Sperrin mountain range is a huge mass of gentle slopes that deceive the onlooker into thinking they are smaller than they are. In fact the peaks rise as high as 683 metres.

The foothills of the mountains are grassy slopes, covered in bogland and rich in heather and other wild flowers. Higher up, they are a mass of streams and small mountain roads, interspersed with the relics of ancient peoples in the form of standing stones and grave slabs from prehistoric times. From the top of the mountains, the views across the landscape of Northern Ireland are exceptional.

There is only a sparse population around this area, adding to the feeling of isolation and space that pervades the Sperrins, and this encourages some of the most unusual wildlife including kestrels and the Irish hare. The range is mainly a haunt for fishermen, and the occasional intrepid person hunting for gold in the mountains. It is a place of magic and wonder, of ancient stillness; a place where time seems to have stood still.

Frosty Morning
CO. DUBLIN

Although the heart of Dublin is a thriving, busy city centre, away from the humdrum of city life, there are many beautiful areas that reflect the general sumptuousness of the countryside all over Ireland. One of the most striking elements about the country is the sense of space, of cleanliness and the feeling of peace that pervades it wherever one goes.

Bordered by the counties of Meath, Kildare and Wicklow, Dublin's outskirts are encroached upon by some of the loveliest countryside in Ireland. Wicklow, particularly, is renowned for its beauty, and has been christened the Garden of Ireland. The land of Dublin is mostly flat apart from the southernmost regions, which contain the very northern peaks of the stunning Wicklow Mountains. The sun rising here over the grasses of Dublin casts a warm glow over the landscape, sending flashes of light rebounding off the frost that covers the ground, and bathing the land in crisp autumn colours. The snatches of cloud at the top of the photograph here are typical of the country, which is known for its beautiful skies and cloud formations. It is a perfect reflection of the beauty that pervades the whole of Ireland.

Lettermore
CO. GALWAY

This isolated house lies in Lettermore, Co. Galway, an area prized for its incredible beauty. It is a village that holds true to the Gaelic speaking tradition, and takes in some of the wild and rocky landscape that makes up part of the diverse Galway scenery.

The landscape in Galway splits into several types, each with very different characteristics. The limestone that typifies so much of the Irish land, particularly Clare, just to the south, is evident here, along with some of the grassy knolls. The dark silhouette of the hills in the background meets the fabulous clouds that roll past as an accepted part of the Irish climate. This scenery is picture-postcard Ireland. Galway is a mining country, and yields not only the limestone that protrudes up from the ground in landscapes like this, but also gravel and marl. Both black and red marble are also quarried in various parts of the county, and this is one of the major industries, apart from fishing that has made Galway as commercially successful as it is.

TOWN LIFE

The towns and cities of Ireland are a welcoming combination of the contemporary bustle of everyday life and the many traditional pastimes and events that have become an inextricable part of Irish culture.

The River Lee
CO. CORK

The River Lee has its source in the beautiful lake of Gougane Barra Park. From here it flows down through the middle of many picturesque villages and towns, that thrive on its shores, and gain good fishing from the river. On its journey, the river passes through a variety of changing landscapes, including woodland and barren countryside, and at Geragh, an area of marshy land and woods that are a perfect haven for wildlife.

The main city the Lee passes through is Cork. It lies between two parts of the river, and many of the streets are built on tributaries of the river. The city is set at the head of the Cork Harbour inlet, and is a vital shipping centre for imports of grain, and exports of Irish livestock to other countries.

Cork was originally a religious settlement founded by St Finbar around AD 622. It developed into a larger town when the Danes turned it into a major trading station in the eleventh century, and since that time the town has changed hands many times, belonging variously to Henry II of England, Oliver Cromwell and the Duke of Marlborough. The rich and varied history of this fine, bustling city is reflected in much of its architecture and many of its traditions.

The Grand Canal
CO. DUBLIN

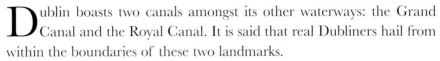

Dublin boasts two canals amongst its other waterways: the Grand Canal and the Royal Canal. It is said that real Dubliners hail from within the boundaries of these two landmarks.

The Grand Canal was formed in 1772, during the period of affluence in which many of the city's grand houses and other structures were built. It was intended to link Dublin with the River Shannon and, thereby, towns in the Irish midlands. It travels through Dublin, right the way down to Robertstown in Co. Kildare, where it splits into two channels, one leading down to the River Barrow in Co. Wexford, the other to Co. Offaly.

These canals became the main channels of trade and transport in Ireland, and throughout the late eighteenth and early nineteenth centuries horses would walk along the tow paths that are still seen by the sides of the canal, pulling the barges with their cargoes of wares, building materials and people. The 1801 Act of Union effectively put a stop to any further developments on the canals, and today they are mainly used for carrying tourists along the waterways to see the countryside and market towns that have sprung up along the canal banks.

Houses near Castleisland
CO. KERRY

It is said that these houses are painted bright colours in order to help their owners find them after a hard night's drinking in the local pub. It is more likely that they simply reflect the pride the Irish have in keeping their surroundings in a state befitting the extraordinary beauty of their country, and their bright, fun-loving nature. All over Ireland, in villages and towns, rows of houses stand out in various vibrant shades.

These houses stand not far from Castleisland in Co. Kerry. The thriving market town takes its name from the castle that used to stand on its spot – 'the Castle of the Island of Kerry'. The castle, erected in 1226 survived nearly 400 years before being destroyed in 1600, and the town still bears its name. The area around here is famous for its impressive limestone cave system, which runs underneath the ground for over two miles, and contains a plethora of strangely shaped stalactites and stalagmites.

Antique Shops
CO. DUBLIN

The city of Dublin is generally divided into two distinct areas: North of the Liffey and South of the Liffey, and ten bridges across the river link these two districts. The town is well-planned, made up of neat suburbs and wide avenues, enhancing the sense of space in a busy urban area. Despite its modern feel, however, there are still parts of Dublin in which one can get a taste of the great history that is partially concealed behind its contemporary setting. This is particularly true of the south-west area of Dublin, where there is an abundance of small, cobbled streets lined with houses and shops, with welcoming proprietors, that date from more than one hundred years ago.

Shopping is one of the many pleasures to be found in Dublin, in a variety of shops that combine the modern and the traditional. The real beauty, however, is that in Dublin, every street is punctuated by fascinating historical monuments, or marvellous buildings that reflect some of the city's great cultural heritage.

Irish Music
CO. GALWAY

Gaelic music flourished from medieval times, until the seventeenth century, when the English rulers began to worry that the patriotic lyrics of some of the folk music may have incited nationalistic feeling. As a result much of the music was suppressed and the patronage of many of the aristocratic families fell away. This led to a new tradition in Irish music – that of the travelling musician, who would move around from place to place, seeking his fortunes at the hands of the new English houses.

This is a tradition that has remained a part of Irish music today. Music is not confined to concert halls, but can be heard in most pubs and on the city streets wherever one travels in Ireland. There is no definite instrumental line-up in Irish bands, mostly they improvise on traditional songs and melodies, using a variety of instruments from the well-known fiddle to the melodian, a basic accordion, and including penny whistles and, occasionally, harps. The distinctive sounds of these instruments combine to create the typical Irish sound, and the improvisational style of Ireland's folk music and ballads have charmed visitors for centuries. Pub music is truly a suitable reflection of the rich cultural traditions of this land.

Old Bushmills Distillery
CO. ANTRIM

The practice of distillation was probably brought to Ireland sometime during the sixth century. It originated in the Middle East as a method for making perfumes, but when it reached Ireland, the monks decided to use the process to make strong alcohol, which was produced and consumed locally. By the sixteenth century it was a significant commercial asset, and became a roaring trade. Over the next 300 years, whiskey was being manufactured and shipped abroad, mainly to the United States, in vast proportions. Prohibition after the First World War was the first step in the whiskey recession, which continued with the Irish civil wars, damaging the home trade. Throughout the depression in 1929, many of the distilleries were forced to close down.

Old Bushmills lays claim to being the first licensed distillery in the world, after the government decided to cut down on the illegal production of whiskey and only grant licenses to the large distilleries. Bushmills had been running since 1276, but has only been operating legally since 1608. It continues to produce some of the finest whiskeys in the world from its home in Co. Antrim.

Neary's Pub
CO. DUBLIN

The Irish are a nation who love to socialise, and drinking is as much a part of the Irish culture as the traditional music and dance. The pubs in Ireland are famous the world over for their welcoming atmosphere and their hospitality – as well as for their fine ales and whiskeys.

Within the confines of the city of Dublin there are over 1000 pubs and bars. Many of these lie in the popular Temple Bar region of the city, which has a reputation for combining the traditional – old cobbled streets and 200 year-old-buildings – with the contemporary trends in shopping and eating.

One of the most popular pubs in the old Irish tradition is Neary's, pictured here. The elaborate Victorian decor within the pub, dominated by traditional gas lamps and an excess of mahogany, as well as a magnificent marble bar, creates an atmosphere of luxury and opulence. It was once very popular with performers of the music hall shows that were fashionable in the city, and members of Dublin's extensive literary circle. Today this exotic and friendly pub is frequented by actors and actresses who come from the Gaiety Theatre next door to relax and unwind after their performances.

Street Life
CO. DUBLIN

The city centre of Dublin is a thriving shopping and socialising area. Divided by the turfy waters of the River Liffey, it is a sprawling, marvellously diverse place. About one third of Southern Ireland's population lives in the Dublin area, and the city itself is full of people – many of them young – yet with the same sense of space that characterises many of the larger towns in Ireland. This is perhaps due to the knowledge that wide open spaces and pure country air are never more than a few minutes' drive away.

The city today has grown from a small Viking settlement that was built here in AD 842, on the banks of a small pond at the meeting point of the River Liffey and the River Poddle. These waterways contained high contents of turf, giving the water a dark and murky aspect, and thus giving rise to the name *dubh linn* ('black water') for the encampment. It has grown from these humble origins into not only the Republic of Ireland's capital, but a unique and popular city that every year welcomes thousands of visitors with typically Irish warmth and hospitality.

A Local Pub
CO. CORK

Pubs like this one are to be found all over Ireland, from the largest cities, to the tiniest hamlets. The pubs in Ireland date back to the Middle Ages, the earliest ones originating around 800 years ago. In medieval times, they were popular taverns, or coaching inns. Their most successful time occurred during the seventeenth and eighteenth centuries, when distilling and brewing technology advanced. Later, Victorian affluence led to many more pubs springing up, and also *shebeens*, the illegal drinking houses that appeared and prospered during colonial rule in Ireland.

Since then, pubs and drinking establishments have become an integral part of Irish life and culture, and one of the most enduring institutions in a country that has seen major changes over the years. Irish pubs have a reputation for their convivial atmosphere and excellent brews. It is here that Irish life at its most vibrant can be found, with spontaneous music sessions, traditional dancing and the age-old tradition of story-telling enlivening the scene and making for a welcoming atmosphere. Every pub in Ireland has its own individual characteristics, some are loud and noisy, others are quiet, reflective and picturesque. The pubs in Cork, like the one pictured here, and Kerry are particularly renowned for their attractiveness and friendliness.

Horse Fair
CO. CORK

The most famous breed of horse for which Ireland is renowned is the Connemara. These were romantically believed to have originated from Spanish Arab horses brought over on the doomed Armada. Some of the horses survived the shipwrecks, and interbred with the local Irish horses to create a new strain that was both faster and more beautiful. The other traditional horse that is reared in this country is the Irish Draught, which is a more sturdy, working horse, used to pull the old ploughs and the traditional carts.

Many horse fairs take place annually in various parts of Ireland, and this one, which occurs on 12 July at Buttevant in Co. Cork is one of the most famous. Here, as at the race meets and shows, the atmosphere is one of lively enjoyment. All breeds and standards of horses and ponies are bought and sold, not just the thoroughbreds. The horse fairs draw crowds of people from all over the country, even those who are not participating in the sales, and here they take part in the jostle and banter that characterises these events.

The Dublin Horse Show
CO. DUBLIN

In all, Ireland boasts twenty-seven racecourses. The Dublin Society Showground is at Ballsbridge, just one of four grounds on the outskirts of Dublin, and every August it hosts the Dublin Horse Show – the main event in the equestrian sporting calendar in Ireland. From all over the world, teams and individuals compete in this prestigious event. Countries including Britain, France, Germany and the Netherlands come to prove themselves at the traditional horse show.

The Irish passion for horseracing, showjumping and other equestrian sports is renowned world-wide, and is reflected in their pride in their thorough-

breds. All over the country race meetings and shows take place. One of the most important is the Irish Derby, which is held at Curragh, a racecourse in Co. Kildare. The plain of Curragh is also where many of the stud horses in Ireland are bred and trained, as it is characterised by a large, unenclosed area of over 5000 acres. In typical Irish style, most of the 250 meetings that are held in the country throughout the year are not simply races, but they take on a festival air that attracts all kinds of people, of the gambling fraternity and others.

Kenny's Bookshop
CO. GALWAY

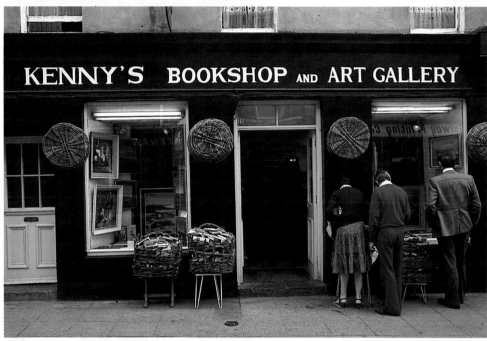

Based in the High Street in the city of Galway, Kenny's Bookshop has become something of a landmark in itself. It comprises five floors of second-hand and antiquarian books and many other curiosities. At the back of the shop is an art gallery that hosts changing exhibitions of Irish art and sculpture, and a print room on the upper floors, which holds a large collection of block prints by Jack Yeats, the artist brother of the famous poet W. B. Yeats. All the items in Kenny's reflect the Irish love of their own culture and history, and the business has been in the hands of the Kenny family for over 50 years.

Kenny's is just one of many fascinating shops in the town of Galway, which is a thriving maritime town, characterised by a bustling atmosphere of friendliness by the locals. There are many places of interest to explore in the town, reminiscent of the town's vital history, and the part it has played in the history of the country.

St Stephen's Square
CO. DUBLIN

St Stephen's Green, in the heart of Dublin, was once an open common, used by locals to cut their firewood, and where livestock was left to graze by the Lord Mayor. It was also where all public executions took place. In 1664, however, it was enclosed, and became a park, with landscaped gardens and lakes.

Today, St Stephen's is a thriving public park, carefully maintained, and dotted with flower gardens, neat paths, ponds and lawns. It is also known for its memorials dedicated to a whole host of famous figures centred around the city, including a Henry Moore statue of W. B. Yeats. The lakes are home to many wild birds, and music is played in the bandstand that was erected in the nineteenth century.

The square is surrounded by the Georgian architecture that characterises much of Dublin, including the fabulous Shelbourne Hotel, which proudly claims to be 'the best address in Dublin'. Today the outskirts of the square are a hive of street traders and musicians, and within the peaceful enclosures, visitors take in the scenery, and students from nearby Trinity College study on the grass.

The Docks
CO. DUBLIN

Dublin is one of the country's major seafaring cities. It grew up at the mouth of the River Liffey on an inlet of the Irish Sea, around Dublin Bay, but it has not always had a seafaring heritage. At the end of the nineteenth century, the boundaries of the city were much further inland, and have been extended throughout the twentieth century.

Today, the Dublin Docks stand on the lower parts of the River Liffey, and are designed with a number of quays to accommodate large vessels. The city is now linked not only with other ports in the Republic of Ireland, but with shipping services in ports throughout England, Scotland and France, as well as Northern Ireland. The port areas are connected to the central River Shannon by the two canals that were built in the city in the eighteenth century. This is the principal port in Ireland, and a major centre for much of the country's trade and commerce. From here products such as the famous Irish whiskey and Guinness are shipped to countries all over Europe and the United States.

Bloomsday
CO. DUBLIN

Bloomsday Celebrations take place annually in Dublin in memory of James Joyce, perhaps the best-known of all Ireland's literary greats. The festival takes its name from the hero of Joyce's masterpiece *Ulysses*, Leopold Bloom. The book traces the thoughts and actions of a day in the life of this character as he walks through the streets of Dublin. Bloomsday is celebrated on 16 June, the same day on which the book is set, in 1904, and people set off to follow Leopold's footsteps through the city. They begin at Prospect Cemetery, where the novel begins, and follow all eighteen sites down to the banks of the River Liffey. Plaques all over the city mark important sites along the way. After the walk, other events include readings of extracts from Joyce's works, and short dramatisations.

Despite the fact that the Irish actually banned the novel in the 1960s, claiming it was pornographic, the festival continues to increase in popularity. Joyce himself claimed to loathe Dublin, yet, despite the fact that he spent much of his life abroad, he could not shake off the influence of the city in which he spent his childhood.

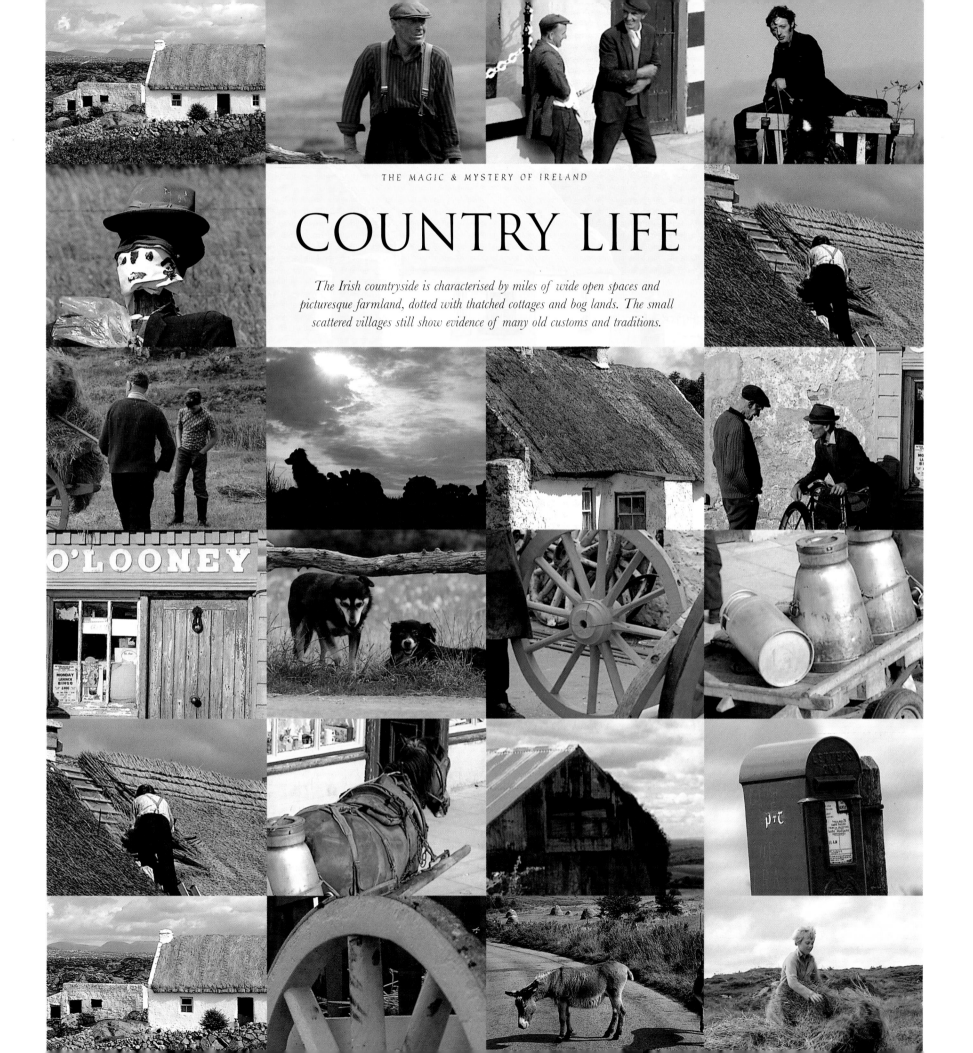

THE MAGIC & MYSTERY OF IRELAND

COUNTRY LIFE

The Irish countryside is characterised by miles of wide open spaces and picturesque farmland, dotted with thatched cottages and bog lands. The small scattered villages still show evidence of many old customs and traditions.

Coachbuilder
CO. MAYO

There is little call for traditional trades such as coachbuilding in Ireland these days. Modern life has taken its toll, and the craftsmen who once made a good living from such trades are now hard to find. Coachbuilding was once an affluent business, when people not only travelled the countryside in carts and coaches, but also used them for work such as carrying turf from the bogs, or hay from the fields. The occasional business such as this can still be spotted in both rural villages and towns in Ireland, but they are few and far between. They cater for the local people who still use horse-drawn carts in the old tradition, and also occasionally for the increasing tourist trade, which offers treks around the countryside and into the mountains on Jaunting Cars as one of its chief attractions.

Tradesmen like this would once have built all kinds of vehicles that were an essential part of everyday life in the country, both for earning a living in the fields, and to travel to the all-important social events that would take place in neighbouring villages.

Stacking Turf
CO. OFFALY

The blocks made from peat or turf cut from local bogs are the main source of fuel in Ireland. In rural areas, men continue this traditional practice of turf-cutting, particularly in areas of Kerry, where the bogs form a large and wildly beautiful part of the landscape.

First the roots and vegetation are stripped away from the surface of the bog, revealing the top layer of peat; this is then divided into narrow strips from which blocks or bricks are cut. When doing this manually, the men use a spade designed for this purpose called a *slean*. This consists of a narrow blade for cutting the turf, with a metal strip at the side to prevent the turf brick from falling off once it has been removed. The bricks are laid out carefully on the surface of the bog to dry out, and are turned and upended until completely dry. They remain stacked up on the bog, often covered in straw or hay, throughout the winter. In the spring they are carried back to the villages and towns to be used for fuel.

Bog land around villages throughout Ireland can often be seen covered in piles of peat bricks at various stages of this process, and men can also be seen cutting the turf in this traditional way, although more modern methods of mechanised peat extraction have been available for a number of years.

Cloghane
CO. KERRY

Cloghane lies at the foot of the Holy Mountain Brandon. Here there is an unusual pilgrim's path that is marked all the way up by the stations of the cross – depictions of Christ's last journey carrying his crucifix. At the top of the mountain, in a place of homage, there is an unusual metal cross, constructed out of the pieces of a German fighter plane which came down on this spot during World War II. Other than this contemporary relic of recent history, Cloghane boasts another, much older, relic from the past. In the Loch a'Duin valley situated close to this quiet town, archeologists have discovered one of the finest series of Bronze Age monuments ever excavated. The valley stretches for 1500 acres, and lying here are nearly one hundred stone monuments dating from all periods of history, as far back as 2500 BC. There are also miles of ancient stone walls that have been covered and preserved by the peat build-up of thousands of years.

The town of Cloghane is situated in one of the quieter parts of the Dingle Peninsula, and is famed for its miles of beautiful beaches stretching to Derrymore. It is a fascinating contrast to the south-western parts of the peninsula which are characterised by rocky landscapes.

Turf Wagon
CO. GALWAY

The turf wagon was once used to transport the peat blocks that had been carefully cut and dried from the bog lands on which they had spent the winter, to the villages and towns, where they were used for fuel in domestic fires. Today, however, these lovely traditional Irish vehicles are rarely seen, even in rural areas.

Pulled by horses or donkeys, the turf wagon was manned by a driver who would master the winding lanes expertly, careful not to lose any of the blocks that had been gained with such hard labour. Although peat is still the major source of fuel in Ireland, it is manufactured by large companies, and most people now buy the peat blocks for their fires from the shops. In some rural areas, however, particularly here in Galway, men still dig in the bogs for their own peat, and these turf wagons can still occasionally be seen coming from the bogs. They are a fascinating part of Irish tradition that is sadly slowly becoming obsolete.

Making Hay
CO. DONEGAL

Although much of the land in Donegal is infertile, making it impossible to grow anything, there are other parts that are more receptive to crop growing, and farming remains just one of the industries that Donegal has to offer. The other major industry today is the manufacture of linens and muslins, trades that began in the cottages but have now extended to deal with the commercial demand for genuine 'home-produced' materials. The location of Donegal has meant that much of it is largely unexplored and unspoilt, and some say that the scenery here is the best in the country. The weather, as in much of Ireland, is extremely changeable, but the general warmth and moistness of the climate makes for good crop-growing.

It is mostly in the further corners of the county that one stumbles across the idyllic sight of stacks of hay, gathered after the harvest and kept for the horses. To go with this picture-postcard scenery, there are thatched cottages in abundance, often white-washed and carefully maintained, adding to the grace and serenity of the Donegal countryside.

Milk Cart

CO. TIPPERARY

A customary Irish scene, this photograph shows milk being carted to the dairy on a traditional two-wheeled cart pulled by a horse. The men stand at the side, passing the early morning in idle yarn-spinning. Today, milk is rarely transported in this way but, as with many other old customs, they can occasionally be glimpsed, a warm shadow of old Ireland that has not quite disappeared.

Today, Ballyporeen, where this picture was taken, is a virtual ghost town. It had a brief moment of fame when it was visited by the American ex-President Ronald Reagan. Reagan, like many Americans, has Irish ancestry, and in 1984 he traced his back to the tiny village, and discovered that Ballyporeen was his ancestral home. The brief moment in the public eye gave Ballyporeen five minutes of fame, but it has returned to its quiet, unobtrusive ways since that time. It is a tiny place now, with a few shops and a village church, but its lack of grandeur only enhances its appeal.

Farmland
CO. CLARE

The famous Clare skies are pictured here over a traditional Irish landscape. In between the harsh borders of the Slieve mountains and the barren limestone pavements of the Burren, Co. Clare is surprisingly hilly and green. There is a predominance of pastures that are used in general for rearing cattle, and large areas of woodland. Particularly around Ennis, the county's capital, there is much farmland like this, edged with the traditional dry stone walls, and flecked with wildflowers that grow in the cracks of the walls and in the fallow pastures and the foothills.

The unspoiled beauty of Clare is a feature of which locals are very proud, and it is something they struggle to maintain. The county is dotted with small farming communities, and the lush greenery of this central area is in stark contrast to the rocks and crags that lie on all sides. The very fact that this part of Clare is surrounded by the infertile, harsh rocky terrain has worked in its favour in the past, for during times of invasion by the Normans throughout the country's history, the invaders found Clare too barren a land to encroach upon. As a result, many of the traditional customs, lifestyle and language have survived better than elsewhere in the country.

Traditional Cottages
CO. GALWAY

The ancient cottages are becoming an increasingly less frequent sight throughout the Irish countryside, as they fall into disrepair and are not restored. They were once used by farm labourers, and were mainly built from wood and clay, occasionally stone. These cottages were very basic, and consisted of just one room, in a rectangular shape. The workers would live in relative squalor while their landlords thrived in disproportionately luxurious country mansions.

The interior of the cottages would vary according to the region in which they were found: in eastern parts, the fireplace and doorway would be aligned, whereas in the western regions, the hearth would 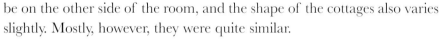 be on the other side of the room, and the shape of the cottages also varies slightly. Mostly, however, they were quite similar.

A few of these cottages remain to give details about the lives of the working classes. Today, the cottages that are built are often modelled on the same style, with perhaps a partitioning wall in the interior. As such they are a picturesque reminder of Irish history, as well as adding to the beauty of the landscape.

POST BOX
CO. WESTMEATH

Westmeath is a largely rural part of the country, famed for its herds of cattle that are reared for beef, and with agriculture as its main industry. Other rural occupations in the area include potato farming and the rearing of livestock. It is a beautiful, unspoilt county, dominated by large areas of water in the form of lakes – particularly Lough Ree, its largest expanse of water – rivers, ancient canals, and streams, all making their way to eventually meet with the mesmerising River Shannon.

In the 681 square miles that the county spans, there are a few towns of note, the largest of which is Athlone, standing at one of Ireland's most central points, straddling the River Shannon. Athlone was once a strategic point marking the boundaries of Connacht and Leinster, and was the site of a major bombardment in the late seventeenth century, which caused much damage to the town, so much so, that its centre was moved from the west to the east bank of the river, where it remains today.

Westmeath is one of the most untouched places left in Ireland today, and remnants of past rural life such as this post box standing in the fields on the outskirts of Athlone, can still be seen adorning the landscape.

Scarecrow
CO. KERRY

Kerry is made up of the kind of film-like, spectacular scenery that many consider to be typically Irish: dark purple mountains, clear lakes, a wild, rocky coastline and vivid green hills. It is largely a region of grandiose mountains, and romantic lakeland settings, but to the north of the county lies a large amount of farmland. Here, characterised by the soft gold of fields of oats and barley, the land is toiled to make a living, and scarecrows like this one are a familiar sight in fields across most of the arable land in Ireland.

Although the landscape here is less dramatic and exciting than in many other parts of the county, particularly the rocky coastline of the Dingle Peninsula, which is Kerry's most popular tourist spot, the northern fields of Kerry have their own special attractions: here there are many relics of the time when the Anglo-Normans dominated the county, in a glorious abundance unseen in other parts of the county.

Connemara
CO. GALWAY

The thatched, whitewashed cottage surrounded by a landscape of dry stone walls and limestone rocks is one that is typical of the Connemara area of Co. Galway. The capital city of the area, Clifden, shares this kind of scenery, set on a rocky inlet above the sea, exposed to the harsh winds and salty sea air that comes in from the Atlantic. In this wildly beautiful place, near Lettermore in Connemara, the people once tried desperately to farm the unyielding earth, Made up from mostly soft bog lands or harsh mountains and limestone crags, the soil is particularly poor, and attempts to tame it have failed. The Great Famine hit this area very hard. Today, however, this uncultivated landscape makes for a beautiful and undisturbed part of the country.

One can walk for many miles in Connemara, coming across only a few desolate cottages and the stunning silvery outcrops of granite and limestone. It is a wilderness of rocks, ideal for exploring. The stillness and silence that this area affords and the breathtaking freedom of large expanses of space, filled only by the wide sky, make this a place that is without time or age.

Thatching the Local Pub
CO. GALWAY

There are only around 2500 thatched cottages left in Ireland today, and over 500 of these are found in Connacht. Once the most popular and traditional methods of roofing a building, thatch has now become a rare sight, and in order to encourage people to repair and maintain their thatched roofs, the state has offered grants to help, and issued advice on methods of maintenance for situations such as this in Galway, showing the local pub being thatched.

Thatch is attached to the roof of a house with ropes using three different methods: scallop, tied or thrust thatching. The straw is twisted into a ball called a *sugan*, then attached to a peg that is placed under the eaves of the house. The rolled-up ball of twisted straw is thrown over the top of the house to the other side, where it is attached to another peg fixed to the rear wall of the house. The latticed mesh of *sugan* is then pegged to the ends of the cottage to keep it firm. This can be a difficult task, and one requiring a number of helpers, but the traditional effect it has at the end is worth the hard work, and the Irish are encouraged to adopt this method of roofing on their buildings, even pubs!

Donkeys
CO. KERRY

Donkeys are as much a part of the Irish landscape as the horses that are bred, reared and trained in this country. Donkeys like this can be seen wandering free in the lanes and fields of many counties. They thrive, like the horses, on the rich grass that is produced by the changeable weather – wet, but warm – to be lush and green.

On a more domestic level, donkeys play their part in the rural activities of the country. Once they would have pulled ploughs, and they are still employed to pull the few carts and coaches that remain, although this is a practice that is becoming less and less necessary, even in the most traditional areas of Ireland.

The sight of animals roaming free across the countryside is a typical country scene, but there is something essentially Irish about having to slow down for donkeys as they pass by. There are wild and reared donkeys, just as there are wild and reared horses, and these can be found mainly on the lowland plains.

Bringing the Turf Home
CO. KERRY

The turf that came from the numerous boglands throughout Ireland was used many years ago for a variety of purposes including cattle litter, manure and as a fuel. Today, it is still the country's major natural resource for fuel, because it is easily accessible, and inexpensive to cut and manufacture. The peatlands that provide these turf blocks, however, are much diminished, and it is estimated that the supply will not last beyond another century.

Turf is not only extracted and manufactured in large quantities by fuel companies, but is also cut and used by individuals living near the bogs, who toil in the peatlands making their own peat bricks, and it is a common sight in the villages of Ireland to see the peat bricks stacked up outside the cottages ready for use.

Before the modern age of technology – largely in the form of heavyweight tractors designed to be able to master the marshy bog land – the peat was carried back from the bogs on donkeys using panniers strapped to them made of wicker. Even today, turf wagons like this one can occasionally be seen making their journey back to the villages piled high with peat blocks that would be used to provide roaring fires and fill rooms with the warmth and the distinctive smell that this natural resource supplies.

O'Looney's
CO. CLARE

This traditional thatched village shop lies in central Clare, and is a rural scene typical for the county. Yet another place where the great diversity of landscape and climate plays its part in Ireland, Clare offers an extraordinary combination of harsh rock and green hills.

The centre of Clare is characterised by a soft and lush countryside and farming land. Many of these small villages can be found around this area. They often have only one or two small shops, and a village church, and also, the ever-present village pub. Together, these few amenities would provide the hub of social activity in these rural areas, where locals would meet for a chat and a drink. Largely, this is all that is needed in the country. The farmers work hard, particularly in Clare where the ground is not always the best soil for agriculture, and self-sufficiency has been a characteristic of Clare people, who have toiled hard to make the county inhabitable for many centuries.

HIGH CROSSES & STANDING STONES

A familiar sight in the Irish landscape is the Celtic high cross silhouetted against the skyline. These, together with the mysterious standing stones and carved grave-slabs, have become a fascinating and valuable part of Irish history.

Cross at Roundstone
CO. GALWAY

The high crosses are one of the most attractive and striking monuments to be seen in Ireland, and there are over 300 of them scattered throughout the Irish landscape. Most of these were built between the seventh and twelfth centuries, and were erected on monastic lands as both a protective symbol and a point of worship.

The earliest stone crosses were carved with simple geometric patterns, but as the art developed, the carvings grew more lavish. Scenes from biblical tales and Christian symbols were inscribed with great detail and accuracy, and were intended as sermons to the masses who would see them. The ring around the top – which has become characteristic of the Celtic cross – has been subject to a number of interpretations, including a halo intended to represent Christ, and a victor's laurel wreath around the Christian *chi-rho* symbol reflecting the victory of Christ. Others believe it was originally a structural device intended to strengthen the cross. Whatever the reasons for it, these ringed crosses have become inextricably identified with Ireland, and have provided a lasting testimony to the craftsmanship of the unknown people who fashioned them.

Standing Stone at Donegal
CO. DONEGAL

As well as the Celtic high crosses, roughly hewn standing stones such as this one are also a familiar sight on the Irish skyline. These date from before the trend for the crosses emerged, many are pagan monuments, and some may even date back to prehistoric times. The majority, however, are early cross-engraved stones. They are mainly slabs, carved on the surface only, but the engravings are not the crude inscriptions one might expect: many are carved with great skill and delicacy with crosses in ornate patterned surroundings, together with many other symbols.

Many of these standing stones are found around the sites of early monasteries, where they would have played a similar role to the later cross monuments – acting as a protective symbol. Some have also been found along the coastlines and on the islands, where hermits and other religious men would have built their solitary retreats. They also tower mysteriously high on hillsides, sometimes hiding tombs beneath their silent roots. Quite often, these stones are also grave slabs, recording the names of the dead and short prayers.

Standing Stones at Waterville
CO. KERRY

Not far away from Sneem and its megalithic remains, lies the town of Waterville. These standing stones are situated on the outskirts of the town, standing on the top of a hill, surrounded by a grid of dry stone walls and under the silent protection of the hills in the distance.

Waterville is a small place, renowned for its excellent fishing. Nearby, on the shore of Ballingskelligs Bay is one of the most beautiful lakes in the country, Lough Currane. The lake is dotted with islands of various sizes, and on one of these lies Waterville's other main relic – although of a slightly later age: a twelfth-century church, which was built in honour of St Finan, who lived during the sixth century. There is also a beehive hut that is said to have been the home of the saint himself. The island is aptly named Church Island.

Waterville itself is surrounded by beautiful beaches, with walks along the coastline and rivers, and through the hills. It is while exploring such places that one can experience the joy of stumbling across pagan standing stones such as these.

Standing Stones at Glencolumbkille
CO. DONEGAL

This small village set on the harbour at Glen Bay on the edge of the Atlantic Ocean is a pilgrim's paradise. It takes its name from *Glenn Cholm Cille*, meaning 'St Columba's Glen', and is a place of homage to one of Ireland's most fascinating saints.

St Columba was a Christian missionary, born in Donegal in AD 521, and is believed to have lived here at Glencolumbkille with a group of his disciples during his lifetime. He had a reputation for being a passionate man, temperamental but contrite, devout yet human, and as such is one of the most popular saints in Ireland; he still has large following.

The standing stone pictured here is just one of over 40 monuments that are scattered around this extraordinary and unusual village. They include not only stones such as this, engraved with curious circular patterns, but also carved cross stones, cairns and crosses. Although many of these monuments date from pre-Christian times, they have all become associated with the legends of St Columba, and the pilgrimage that takes place annually on 9 June makes a tour of fifteen of these stations. This eclectic collection of carved stonework provides an unexpected mass of fascinating history in this small town.

Cross at Monasterboice
CO. LOUTH

The high crosses are the most spectacular part of the monastic settlement at Monasterboice. The settlement was founded by St Buite, a disciple of St Patrick in AD 520, and the site also bears evidence of two churches, a round tower and two very early grave-slabs.

The three high crosses date from the tenth century, and are remarkably well-preserved, particularly the cross of Muiredach, pictured here. This stands at 5.5 metres high, and is covered with detailed and ornate carvings of biblical scenes, most impressively, the Last Judgement which covers the whole of the eastern face of the cross-head. On either side of the Judgement Throne are inscribed images of the Blessed and the Damned, and it is a superb example of a scripture cross.

The remaining two crosses that can be found here have suffered more from erosion, but much of their delicate stone-carving can still be seen, and it is an appropriate testimony to the craftsmen who built these monuments that they have stood for hundreds of years, to the admiration of all those who visit Monasterboice.

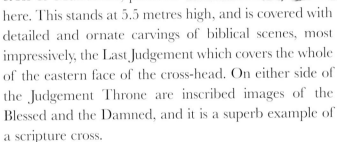

Cross of the Scriptures at Clonmacnoise
CO. OFFALY

Three complete high crosses were found at the site of the ancient monastic settlement at Clonmacnoise, founded by St Ciaran in the sixth century. In addition, the relics of a number of others are dotted around. The north and south crosses are fairly well-worn, although some of the ornate carvings can still be made out. The jewel of this site, however, is the Cross of the Scriptures.

Clonmacnoise itself may have been one of the original sources of the Celtic High Cross, and it is believed that there was a workshop here for sculpting. The Cross of the Scriptures is one of the most magnificent results of this. It was erected in the early tenth century for the king of Ireland, Flann Sinna, and is marvellously decorated with carved patterns and figures. It is now difficult to identify these figures accurately although there are a number of theories attached to each one. The Cross is divided into carved panels on all four sides. The west side, photographed here, shows a number of scenes, possibly including the Flagellation (directly beneath the cross head) and the arrest of Christ (second panel down). Inscriptions on the east and west faces indicate the name of King Flann, and this has helped date the Cross to approximately AD 900.

Grave Slab at Clonmacnoise
CO. OFFALY

Grave slabs such as this one are another relic of the past that can be found at monastic sites and ancient graveyards throughout Ireland. Although less durable than many of the immense dolmen and high crosses, and much worn by time, they still provide a fascinating insight into early stone carving practices, and the history of the areas in which they are found.

There are over 200 gravestones at the site at Clonmacnoise, both upright and recumbent, and they cover a time span of many centuries, from the pagan era to the present day. Clonmacnoise was the last resting place of many great figures such as the kings of Connacht, and the inscriptions of the grave slabs often tell names and dates, sometimes in Gaelic, although more frequently they are simply inscribed with crosses. The style of these crosses varies: some are carved in the Greek style, within a circle, others take the form of a Latin cross characterised by its square-ended arms. They were often enhanced by beautiful decorative scrolls and geometric patterns.

The largest collection of grave stones at Clonmacnoise is found by the entrance to the site, and these date from between the sixth and eleventh centuries. From a distance, these stones give an ancient, ethereal feel to a place that contains a wealth of silent history within its boundaries.

Drombeg Stone Circle
CO. CORK

There would once have been seventeen standing stones forming this prehistoric circle. Only thirteen of them remain today, but this is sufficient to provide a visitor with an immense sense of awe at the ancient site. Dating from the second century BC, Drombeg is known locally as the Druid's Altar – a name commonly given to the standing stones and dolmen that are a familiar characteristic of the Irish countryside.

The circle stands roughly nine metres in diameter, and the stones are made from smooth local sandstone. The entrance to the circle is marked by two upright portal stones and faces a recumbent altar stone. This is arranged so that on the midwinter sunset, the rays of the sun will fall directly on to it, when viewed through a point in the distant hills. When the site was excavated in the 1950s, cremated human remains were found in a pot near the centre of the circle.

Cork was once the centre of Neolithic life and worship in Ireland, and evidence of this remains near Drombeg: two stone huts dating from this era lie just to the west, and an ancient cooking pit was found in a nearby stream, where stones heated from a fire would have been placed to heat water.

Cross at Drumcliff
CO. SLIGO

Just outside the churchyard where the poet W. B. Yeats is buried in Co. Sligo, lie a few scattered remains of a monastic site founded in AD 575 by Columkille. One of the most impressive of these remains is a magnificent tenth-century high cross.

Although the cross is quite worn, it is still possible to see the marks of a wealth of carvings and inscriptions on all sides. The biblical scenes carved on the cross include Adam and Eve on the east face, along with Cain and Abel, Daniel in the Lion's Den and the Last Judgement. The western face of the cross shows the Presentation in the Temple and the Crucifixion. Other carvings are less clear, and could be interpreted as a number of Old and New Testament stories. All these carvings are interlaced with exquisitely delicate scrollwork and inscriptions. The cross stands at nearly four metres high, and is made of sandstone with pellet mouldings on its faces. It forms just part of a fascinating historic area of this part of the country.

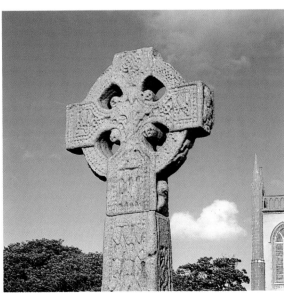

CROSS AT SNEEM
CO. KERRY

Sneem is a bright village lying on the Ardsheelaun River in Co. Kerry. It is surrounded by stunning river scenery and is backed by the formidable mountain range of the Cahas. The village and the surrounding area are also scattered with archeological relics such as this high cross. Other monuments include a fascinating hermitage that is hewn from solid rock, which is said to belong to St Crohane.

Sneem's most renowned monument, however, is the ruin of Staigue Fort that lies a few miles away from the village itself. This is a magnificent and imposing relic, circular in shape and built from stones without the use of any mortar at all. The staircases inside the fort are still near to perfect despite the ages that have passed since it was constructed.

The ruins that lie scattered around this village are a dominant feature of the landscape, and sights such as the high cross are an intrinsic element of the beautiful scenery of shimmering water and dark, looming mountains that make up this part of the county.

Browne's Hill Dolmen
CO. CARLOW

The Irish countryside is dotted with the mysterious shapes of the prehistoric dolmen. Taken from two Breton words meaning 'stone table', these ancient monuments have survived the ravages of time to tell the modern world of a near-forgotten era of pagan rituals and worship.

The Browne's Hill dolmen is perhaps the most awe-inspiring of the all the dolmen that stand on the plains of Ireland. It dates back to 2000 BC, and is believed to be a giant megalithic tomb, possibly the last resting-place of a local chieftain. It is also likely to have been a place where religious rites were enacted, and it is possible that as part of these rituals, human sacrifices were made.

Its most impressive feature, however, is its sheer size: the dolmen is made up of a huge granite capstone lying across two portal stones flanking a door-stone. It is embedded in the earth at one end, and leans westwards supported by a large boulder at the other. The capstone is allegedly the largest stone in Europe – there is no doubt that it is the largest in Ireland – weighing an almighty 150 tonnes. Exactly how a monument of such massive proportions would have been constructed in prehistoric times will probably remain a mystery for ever.

CROSS AT DYSERT O'DEA
CO. CLARE

Standing conspicuously intact and impressive amongst the ruins of this ancient monastic settlement in Dysert O'Dea, the high cross is one of the most important monuments in Co. Clare. Lying just to the east of the remains of the old church, it certainly dominates this particular site.

Dating from the mid-twelfth century, this is one of the finest examples of the last phase in high cross art and sculpture. The cross does not have the ring that characterises many Celtic crosses, and it is carved from grey limestone – a material that would have been freely available locally in the county.

It is perhaps best known for its striking and unusual design: the base of the north face depicts the founding of the church, while on the south face a carving telling the biblical tale of Daniel in the Lion's Den is still clearly visible. The east face, showing a high relief carving of the crucifixion, is particularly impressive. The figure of the bishop beneath the crucified Christ may well be St Tole, who founded the monastery at Dysert O'Dea in the eighth century.

Standing Stones at Loughcrew
CO. MEATH

This collection of standing stones is situated on a hill called Loughcrew in Oldcastle, Co. Meath, constituting an impressive and mysteriously exciting site. These stones are one of two sites that lie on the hills to the north-west of Kells – one of the most famous places in Ireland by virtue of its ancient manuscript, the *Book of Kells*, which is now housed at Trinity College in Dublin. These collections of stones have fantastic carvings covering their surfaces in strange ray patterns, and it is believed that the engravings and the position of the stones worked as a primitive calendar for telling the days of the year. To the pagan race that erected these, this would have been important for reasons of both agriculture and religion.

Amidst the stones here on these 250-metre-high hills, are burial chambers, most of which are now carefully locked away from the public for reasons of preservation. Who they were for is unknown. The strange and ancient stones and cairns are subject to much speculation, but it seems likely they will remain a fascinating Neolithic mystery.

Poulnabrone Dolmen
CO. CLARE

The Poulnabrone dolmen stands dramatically in the Burren's limestone pavements. The name means 'the hole of the sorrows', and when this prehistoric tomb was opened in 1968, the remains of nearly thirty Neolithic humans were recovered, including six children, one newborn baby and between sixteen and twenty-two adults. Experiments done on these remains proved that they had been placed in the tomb as bones, indicating that they were buried or laid exposed somewhere else first. The small number of remains found would also indicate that this was perhaps the burial chamber of a particular tribe or family, or the leaders of the community, rather than a general burial site.

Also excavated from the tomb were a significant number of objects that are valuable relics of Neolithic culture in this part of Ireland. Among these were many shards of crude pottery, arrowheads, and items of jewellery. It is possible that these objects formed part of a prehistoric burial ritual.

This fascinating monument is made up of an enormous capstone measuring 365 cm by 213 cm lying on two portal stones of almost two metres high. This creates a chamber of approximately nine metres. The dolmen has been carefully restored and maintained as one of Ireland's most interesting and mysterious sights.

TRADITION & CULTURE

Old Irish traditions have not quite disappeared in the increasingly modern way of life, and all over the country many of the ancient customs and beliefs are maintained and celebrated in everyday life and annual festivities.

Bridge at Graiguenamanagh
CO. KILKENNY

The small market town of Graiguenamanagh stands on the banks of the River Barrow in the Sylvan Valley, which runs along the eastern boundaries of Co. Kilkenny. This lovely town sprang up and spread around the ruins of the ancient Cistercian settlement that once stood on this spot. The most impressive relic of this affluent time is Duiske Abbey, which was built at the turn of the thirteenth century, and was once the largest in Ireland. It is from this that the town gets its name, which means 'granary of the monks'. Although the exterior of the abbey has been significantly altered over the centuries, much of the inside has been preserved in its original form, and the fantastic Romanesque carvings remain as impressive today as they would have been in medieval times.

This picturesque stone bridge crosses the river Barrow with Graiguenamanagh on the far side, and the spot is noted for its outstanding beauty and wildlife: waterfowl, particularly herons frequent the weir, where the fishing is good, and above the town towers the famous Holy Mountain Brandon.

Castlegregory
CO. KERRY

A local chieftain, Gregory Hoare built a castle here in the mid-sixteenth century, at the height of his power and affluence. His son Hugh – in true Romeo and Juliet style – was in love with the daughter of Gregory's oldest and deadliest rival, Will Moore. Hoare and Moore were fighting over the boundaries of their adjacent territories and were the bitterest of enemies. Their children enjoyed a secret love affair out of sight in the peaceful wooded surroundings of the village.

A few years later, however, the law ruled in Moore's favour, and Hoare returned to his castle a ruined man, and soon turned imbecile at the loss of pride in the face of his rival. A short time after Hoare's downfall, Hugh decided to marry Ellen Moore, and on their wedding day, their names were joined in a carving on the limestone arch over the door of the castle. On the same day, Gregory Hoare dropped dead from anger at seeing his arch enemy in his own castle.

Hugh and Ellen's marriage was not a happy one, with Hugh eventually killing his wife, and then dying himself from remorse at what he had done. The castle was burned to the ground by Cromwell's soldiers in 1649, and today there is no trace left of it in Castlegregory, except the limestone carving, with the names of Hugh Hoare and Ellen Moore inscribed on it, which stands in the village centre.

Jaunting Car
CO. KERRY

The Jaunting Car is a method of transport that is unique to Irish history. It was designed in the early nineteenth century, and could carry four passengers and a driver. Cars such as this one, which lies on the Blasket Islands in Co. Kerry, would have been used to carry families to the landing point where they would travel across the water to hear mass on the mainland every Sunday.

The body of the car was mounted on springs, with only two wheels underneath, and two long wooden seats placed lengthways in the back, so the passengers could sit facing out sideways while travelling. In the front, was an elevated driver's seat, although some cars would not be fitted with this luxury. In these cases, the driver would often sit on one of the passenger seats, and control the vehicle from the side, or he would sit uncomfortably on the back of one of these seats. It was not an ideal method of transport for travelling across the often rocky and uneven Irish countryside, and this probably explains its lack of popularity elsewhere.

Although the Jaunting Car is now obsolete, there are reminders of this old-fashioned vehicle spread around the country; wheels can be found rotting on the plains, and broken pieces of the body lie untouched in the grass. Some cars are more well-preserved, and are kept as a fascinating reminder of early nineteenth-century Irish life.

Galway Hooker
CO. GALWAY

These traditional sailing boats were created many years ago and were tailored to meet the needs of local Irish people. They were entirely unlike any other boats of the time. They were built of heavy wood, and had sturdy masts and sails. Thus designed, they were extremely strong, and would weather the worst sea journeys, through the wild waters of the Atlantic.

Originally, they were built to carry peat across to the Aran Islands from Galway, as the islands had none of the peat bogs that dominated the mainland, and they relied solely on these hookers to ferry this life-giving fuel to them. They were also used to carry livestock and beer along the coast when necessary, and occasionally they would transport building materials from one site to another round the coast of Ireland. The pronounced tumblehome, which was one of the main advantages of this design, meant that the boat had less of a keel, protecting the cargo from getting waterlogged – this was clearly essential when carrying peat for fuel.

Local tales tell that all the Galway Hookers would dip their sales in homage as they passed MacDara's Island off the coast of Connemara. MacDara was the Patron Saint of sailors, and until recently, of the Hookers themselves. Today, the Galway Hookers can be seen in action at the annual festival of *Cruinniú na mBad* ('Gathering of the Boats') which takes place in Galway every August.

The Currach
CO. GALWAY

Apart from the hookers, Galway is also famed for its other sea craft, the currach. This has become an essential part of the county's history, and even today the currachs are still used for their original purpose, although they have been adapted and modernised.

The currach has been used on the Galway coasts as a fishing boat, and a method of transporting all manner of cargo, including livestock for many centuries. The first currachs were very small craft and were built by stretching tarred animal skins, particularly cowhide, across frames made of wicker or a heavier timber. Over the years, the boat has been adapted to be able to deal with changing climates and conditions in various regions off the coast, and one of its main characteristics is that the currach has no keel, which allows it to slide across the top of the water, rather than move through it, often making for a smoother journey than most local crafts can provide.

Today, currachs are made from tarred canvas and a frame of wooden lathes, and they are still used both in Galway and in other regions. As with the Hookers, the currachs take part in many local festivals and celebrations, including one on the island of Innishmore, the highlight of which is the currach boat race.

Greyhounds
CO. CLARE

The Irish have a passion for both racing and gambling, and their fondness for both horse racing and greyhound racing reflects this popular pastime. Like the many horse races, however, the appeal of greyhound racing in Ireland is not restricted to an elite group of gamblers, but is increasingly becoming a social event, attracting many people from all over the country.

Greyhounds are bred and trained in Ireland for the purpose of racing, and the export of the dogs to other countries, particularly Britain has become something of a minor industry in itself. The Irish are proud of their talents in this area, just as they are of their famous thoroughbred horses that are renowned the world over.

Greyhound racing is a sport that is growing in popularity and affluence throughout Ireland, and now many towns boast a dogtrack, as prize money and sponsorship deals are fed back into the sport. The most popular race for greyhounds is the Greyhound Derby, which takes place at Shelbourne Park in Dublin in early October every year.

The Harp
CO. WICKLOW

Records of the harp being used as part of traditional Irish music have been found as far back as the eleventh century, and its delicate sound has been a popular part of the musical tradition since this time – to the effect that the harp has now become one of the country's national symbols.

The talents of the Gaelic harpists have been acknowledged all over the world as far back as Renaissance times. Although it experienced a decline in popularity after the sixteenth century, a great harp festival held in Belfast in 1792 brought it back into the limelight, and it was restored as one of Ireland's most significant musical instruments. One of the most

famous Irish harpists was Turlough O'Carolan, who, although blind, travelled around the country during the suppression of traditional Irish music by the English, playing his harp not just in the courts of the wealthy aristocrats, but also for the poor. Many of the songs that have survived as part of Ireland's heritage are attributed to him.

Today the harp is as popular as it ever was, although its soft tones make it impractical for use in the traditional pub bands, but it is often played solo or in small ensembles, and great harpists are again making their name: Mary O'Hara pictured here with her harp, against the stunning backdrop of the lakes at Glendalough, is now one of the most famous contemporary harpists in Ireland.

The Aran Islands
CO. GALWAY

The inhabitants of the Aran Islands have always been a strong, hardy people. Forced to scrape their living toiling the unproductive earth to produce meagre harvests of potatoes, they have survived the wild and unpredictable climate on the islands since prehistoric times.

Because of this, the islanders to this day remain a self-reliant and solitary people. The isolation they have been forced to endure has led to the perpetuation of many ancient customs and beliefs, long after changes had taken place on the mainland. Aran islanders are particularly proud of their race and their traditions, many of which are kept alive today. The islands remain firmly Gaelic speaking, enhancing the ancient

and romantic atmosphere on the islands. This display of religious items in a small house on one of the islands reflects the old-fashioned culture. Christianity was brought to the islands in the sixth century, reputedly by St Edna, and there are a number of old Christian ruins throughout the islands. Mixed in with these, however, is a fantastic array of pagan relics, telling of the rich social and religious ancestry of which the islanders today are so proud.

The Ha'penny Bridge
CO. DUBLIN

This famous landmark links the northern and southern sides of the city of Dublin, from Liffey Street to the popular Temple Bar area, known for its many pubs and cafes lining its cobbled streets.

This arched cast-iron footbridge across the River Liffey in the heart of Dublin was built in 1816 by John Windsor, an ironworker hailing from Shropshire in England. As such, it is one of the earliest structures of its kind made from cast iron. It was originally christened the Wellington Bridge, but now its official title is the Liffey Bridge. The name Ha'Penny Bridge comes from the toll that pedestrians were charged when the bridge first opened until it was discarded in 1919. To confuse matters more, it is also sometimes referred to as the Metal Bridge.

The Ha'Penny Bridge is now one of the most pleasant spots in Dublin, amongst the hub of city life, and work continues to ensure the bridge stays a popular attraction: recently, traditional period lanterns were put on the archways to keep the atmosphere alive.

Painting in Connemara
CO. GALWAY

For many years now, the wild beauty of Connemara has attracted artists, who throng to the area to try and capture the scenery that makes this part of Galway one of the most memorable places in the country.

The landscape is diverse, made up of lush green hills running into blue and white mountains, dotted with the rainbow colours of hundreds of species of wild flowers that spring up in hedgerows, fields and hollows. Connemara is dominated by water, in the form of lakes and rivers, streams and pools, all of which add to the illusionary feel of the area. The colours and shadows are constantly shifting, light and dark merge and change, at times there seem to be no boundaries between the sky and the mountains, the mountains and the rolling foothills, the hills with the placid waters that in turn reflect the sky. It is a circle of beauty. This has proved to be an inspiration not just for painters – amateur and professional alike – but also for creative people from all areas including writers, poets, playwrights and craftsmen. It is one of the most ideal places in Europe to sit in solitude and reflect, and capture, the atmosphere of Ireland.

Natural Stone Walls
CO. GALWAY

The playwright John Millington Synge, a regular visitor to the Aran Islands described them as 'a wilderness of stone and stone walls', and all three of the islands are dominated by these natural stone walls. The land of the islands is harsh and stony, unproductive and lacking in soil. The islanders have toiled this infertile land for many centuries, braving the harsh Atlantic winds and the exposed elements to scrape a meagre living.

The walls that can still be seen in a criss-cross pattern all over the islands were erected to protect the land from the Atlantic gales. They also helped to clear the fields of the rocks from which the land is made up. The fields that they surround are tiny in comparison with the mainland crop fields, and the farmers would have to manufacture their own soil from rotting seaweed to encourage anything to grow in the tough earth.

On Inishmaan, an island less than three miles in length, where this picture was taken, these stone walls are larger and more impressive than on the other two islands. Here, they may stand to six feet high, and, being covered in yellow moss, lack the dull grey of others, with a glow that detracts from an otherwise barren, cold landscape.

Holy Well
CO. CLARE

Holy wells are just some of the objects of veneration and homage that draw hundreds of people to certain places in Ireland every day. They can be seen in abundance all over the country, particularly in Co. Clare where this one stands. The wells normally have specific saints associated with them (Ireland has a plethora of saints, who patronise many different causes), and people travel some distance to pay homage at these places.

The wells generally have magical attributes as well. The waters within each well are often said to cure certain diseases. Drinking water from St Senan's Well, for example, is said to cure blindness, St Brigid's Well will allegedly cure all ills, and is a place of pilgrimage on Garland Sunday at the end of July, when people will come to take the waters of the well, and relieve themselves of everything from headaches to more serious diseases. This is an age-old tradition in Ireland, so much so that the famous Irish playwright John Middleton Synge wrote a play entitled *The Well of the Saints*, based on a story told to him about a certain well on the Aran Islands.

Kate Kearney's Cottage
CO. KERRY

The infamous Kate Kearney ruled her small part of Killarney in the mid-nineteenth century. She was a local girl, and renowned for being a great beauty, and a shrewd business woman, by all accounts. She would entice travellers through the town into her house, and sell them illegal moonshine, or poteen, which she brewed herself. As a result, she was continually having run-ins with the local law-enforcement, but this did not detract from her success.

As the last chance of obtaining food and drink before travellers would approach the famous Gap of Dunloe, Kate was almost guaranteed a roaring trade. The Gap was the route through the mountains, with the Macgillcuddy Reeks on one side and the Purple Mountain (so called because of its abundance of heather) on the other. It was seven miles across the Black Valley before the next watering hole. Nearly all travellers would take advantage of Kate's 'hospitality' to fortify their strength and their courage.

Kate prospered until the Great Famine deprived her of the potatoes that were so essential for the distilling of poteen. Exactly what happened to her is unknown, as she just disappeared mysteriously one night, never to be seen again.

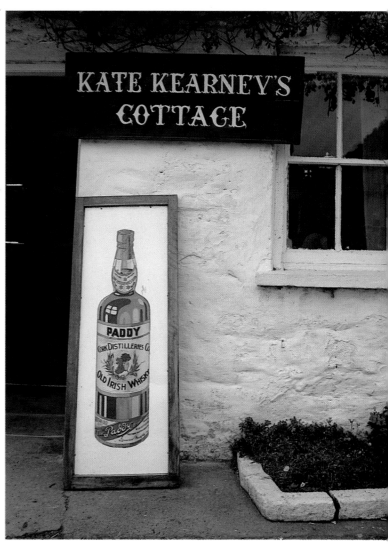

Polo in Phoenix Park
CO. DUBLIN

As well as the landscaped gardens and wilderness areas of Phoenix Park on the outskirts of Dublin city, the park includes sports grounds which are used in all seasons. Polo is one of the most popular of these sports, and polo matches can be seen in Phoenix Park throughout the summer months, drawing crowds who sit in the captivating surroundings enjoying the spectacle.

Two of the more traditional Irish games that also take place here are Gaelic football and hurling. Gaelic football combines elements of rugby and Australian Rules Football, and is a fast, often rough, game. Although it is popular throughout Ireland, it is especially worshipped in Donegal. Hurling, a very traditional Irish sport played with sticks, is a mixture of hockey and lacrosse, and is believed to have been played as far back as Celtic times in Ireland. Organised events of both these sports are arranged by the Gaelic Athletic Association, an institution founded over 100 years ago, in an attempt to encourage traditional Gaelic sports, and discourage British influences. Like many Irish sports, hurling is played at local and county levels, and finals take place in Dublin to audiences of vast numbers.

Fishing in Galway City
CO. GALWAY

The city of Galway was founded by the Normans in the middle of the thirteenth century, although the area itself had been inhabited since pre-Christian times. The Norman chieftain actually gave the city to the charge of fourteen of his supporters and their families to keep and defend against the local Irish tribes, and these families and their descendants did so effectively until long after Norman ascendancy had declined in the area.

One of the most impressive features of Galway City is the River Corrib. This flows down from the great Lough through the city and into the ocean. The river has a colony of the famous mute swans, which can be seen floating gracefully down the river – a truly spectacular sight. The other thing for which the river is famed is its salmon shoal. From the middle of April through to the beginning of July, the salmon can be seen lying in the water under the Salmon Weir Bridge, gathering to start their journey back from the ocean upstream to lay their eggs in the cool of Lough Corrib. As a seafaring city, fishing has been a popular pastime, since Galway City was first settled, and anglers can still be seen up and down the edges of the River Corrib.

Guinness Advertisement
CO. TIPPERARY

The dark beer with its smooth, creamy head, has become a symbol as much identified with Ireland as the shamrock. Local legend tells that in 1759 the young brewer Arthur Guinness burned a batch of barley while brewing the local ale, so he gave away the resulting drink, thinking it was unsaleable. The customers who had taken it were back clamouring for more within days, and its popularity has spread world-wide since then. It is, however, more likely that Arthur Guinness heard of a black ale that was being produced in London, under the name of porter and decided to experiment with his own recipe in an attempt to revive the failing brewing industry in Ireland.

Whatever the origins of this beer, though, it is now one of the best-selling beverages. The Guinness Brewery in St James's Gate in Dublin covers a massive sixty-four acres to the south of the River Liffey. The brewery produces four million pints every day, and these are shipped to 120 countries all over the world. Advertisements for the stout have been seen throughout the country, since the very first advertisement announced that 'Guinness is Good for You'.

Beehive Huts
CO. KERRY

These unusual huts can be found scattered all over Co. Kerry, occasionally they are isolated, sometimes they form part of a community of houses, now barren and deserted for many centuries. The beehive huts – or *clochons* – are fine examples of this ancient architectural style, mostly built between the sixth and eighth centuries. To see them now, one wonders how they have survived as well as they have, for they look very susceptible to the elements, and here on the Dingle Peninsula in Co. Kerry, the wind can be harsh.

The huts were built originally for sheltering both livestock and people, and pilgrims travelling to the many places of worship throughout Ireland, would rest here in the darkness and solitude to pray and sleep. The huts are created by building up layers of stone in a fashion called *corbelling*; this simply means laying each series of stones so it projects beyond the layer below. Unusually, however, these huts were built without the use of mortar to steady the stonework and fill the gaps through which the wind whistled.

Pilgrims can still make the walk up the hillside to the villages in Kerry, or visit the isolated community on the crag of Skellig Michael, which forms a very primitive monastery. The beehive villages remain one of the most fascinating bequests from the early Irish people, from a time when little architecture has survived intact.

Statue of Molly Malone
CO. DUBLIN

In Dublin's fair city where the girls are so pretty
I first set my eyes on sweet Molly Malone.
She wheeled a wheelbarrow through streets broad and narrow
Crying 'cockles and mussels, alive, alive O!'

The large statue of Molly Malone stands at the south end of Grafton Street in Dublin, which stretches through the city centre from Trinity College, and is one of the most popular shopping streets in Dublin. It is a monument erected in honour of the heroine of one of Ireland's most famous traditional songs – *The Ballad of Molly Malone*. Molly was a street trader, peddling her wares of cockles and mussels in Fishamble Street, the site of a prospering medieval fish market. The ballad tells how 'she died of a fever, no one could relieve her', and it is likely that she caught typhoid from eating seafood from Dublin Bay, which would have been very polluted.

The life-sized statue, fashioned from bronze, was created by Jean Rynhart, and shows Molly wheeling her barrow, peddling her wares. Legend has it that the ghost of poor Molly Malone still walks the streets of Dublin.

Statue of Daniel O'Connell
CO. DUBLIN

O'Connell Street is justifiably Dublin's most famous road. It was designed in the eighteenth century to be a fashionable residence for people of means. It is a wide thoroughfare, with a parade down the middle that is lined with statues and memorials.

Originally named Sackville Street, it was renamed in 1892 after Daniel O'Connell, also known as The Liberator. O'Connell hailed from an Irish Catholic family, and broke free of his family's trades (which included smuggling!) to become a lawyer and later a politician. In 1823, he set up the Catholic Association, and with the money he earned from the membership dues, he sowed the seeds of a major new political force. When, in 1828, the county of Clare elected him with a vast majority, parliament at Westminster was forced to change the bill that refused Catholics the right to sit as members, for fear of riots in Ireland from his army of supporters. O'Connell thus forged a new path that would lead to Catholic emancipation.

The statue dedicated to him was sculpted by John Henry Foley in 1882. It depicts O'Connell receiving the 1829 Act of Emancipation from the allegorical figure of Erin, symbolising Ireland. Around the figures, four winged victories, representing Courage, Fidelity, Eloquence and Patriotism, salute the man who changed Irish politics forever.

NATURAL
LANDMARKS

Buried deep below the ground, and towering as high as the holy mountain Croagh Patrick, there are a number of fascinating natural landmarks in Ireland, each one adding to the captivating and unique nature of the Irish landscape.

The Marble Arch Caves
CO. FERMANAGH

These remarkable caves are carved out of the limestone that is found all over Ireland. They contain myriad passages and chambers, all characterised by some of the largest and finest stalagmites found anywhere in the world.

Three streams run through the caves, from the Cuilcach Mountain. These are also the source of the River Shannon that flows through most of the Irish countryside. Explorers in the caves can travel right to their heart by boat on these waterways. While exploring the caves, a visitor also comes across waterfalls and a spectacular array of formations made by erosion of the limestone walls and floors. The walls and ground of the caves are sprinkled with minerals and rocks, causing them to shimmer magically like something from an ancient fairy tale.

The Marble Arch itself, from which the caves derive their name, stands outside the caves marking the point where the river rushes out from the caves. These are a marvellous sight hidden away in the very depths of the Fermanagh earth.

The River Liffey
CO. DUBLIN

The Liffey is the most important landmark in Dublin. It cuts through the centre of the city, dividing it into two distinctive regions, north and south of the river. Along the banks of the Liffey lie some of the most magnificent pieces of architecture in the country including the Custom House and the Four Courts. There are ten bridges that cross the river in Dublin, including the famous Ha'Penny Bridge. The river widens out towards the port and eventually flows into the ocean. Due to the abundance of peat land in Ireland, the river has a dark splendour about its waters. Like most major cities, the river is the main reason for its success, providing a valuable means of transport for trading in days when travel by road was arduous.

The source of the river lies near the approach to Kippure Mountain, whose summit stands at 745 metres. It is not far from the famous military road created in 1798, which runs from Rathfarnham into the mountains. The river wends its way down the mountainside in Co. Kildare, thence heading northwards into Dublin.

Sandy Beach
CO. LOUTH

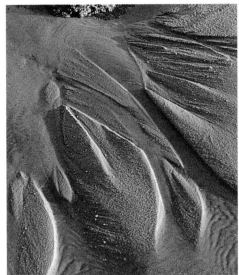

Although the coastlines of Ireland are mainly rocky, characterised by steep cliffs and barren land, the country also has many lovely beach strips (known as strands) in most of its coastal areas. Of the 2000 miles of coastline around Ireland, nearly 500 of these miles are made up of sandy dunes. These often consist of tiny grains of quartz or granite – elements of which Ireland has much – which have been carried along by the rivers down to the sea, to be washed up on the beaches. Other strands are small and rocky, covered in shingle, and are places of solitude and reflection against the backdrop of the dramatic Atlantic Ocean and Irish Sea.

The beaches at Louth, pictured here at sunset, are unspoiled by any large resort towns, and are home to many sea birds

who make their nests amongst the dunes, unaffected by human disturbances. The tide rushes in at great speed on many of the Irish beaches, leaving remnants of its aquatic inhabitants and plants amongst the shingles and sands. Often oysters can be found in these coastal regions, and searching for the pearls is just one of the magical experiences these beaches provide.

Rocky Coastline
CO. KERRY

Much of the coastline of Ireland is dominated by sheer cliffs and rocky promontories like these. They are a typical characteristic of the Irish landscape, and a dramatic addition to a country that boasts some of the most marvellous scenery in the world. Crashing interminably on to the rocks is the wild and intimidating Atlantic Ocean. Cliffs like the ones at Moher are some of Ireland's most famous natural landmarks.

Seen here in the distance are the mysterious and fantastic deserted islands of Blasket, thrown off from the dramatic rocky Slea Head promontory. They are themselves characterised by high cliffs and steep rocks, forming an impressive and eerie silhouette against the darkening sky in the pounding waves of the Atlantic.

The mighty rocks that take up such a large part of Ireland's coastline have stood there for many centuries since the island was formed in prehistoric times, and they give the country a wild and untamed aspect, and a dramatic spirit that reflects the island's heritage and history.

The Cliffs of Moher
CO. CLARE

The views from the Cliffs of Moher are unsurpassed, and the cliffs themselves are one of Ireland's most breathtaking landmarks. Typical of the rocky coastline of the country, these cliffs rise 213 metres in sheer height from the sea, and run a length of eight miles along the Atlantic coast on the west of Ireland, from the appropriately named Hag's Head in the south, to O'Brien's Tower in the north.

The face of the cliffs is made up of thousands of layers of sandstone and shale, and on the sheltered ledges these provide, many different birds can be found nesting in the spring, including guillemots and shags. Even puffins inhabit this area in the spring. In the winter, the cliffs form part of an eerie barren landscape, shrouded in mists with the only sounds to be heard, the howling of the wind from the nearby Burren plains, and the relentless pounding of the forces of the sea below. There are no fences protecting people from the cliff edges, so there is nothing to spoil the dangerously spectacular view down to the sea from the cliffs. The seclusion and wildness of this place is timeless.

The Burren
CO. CLARE

The 116 square miles of rough limestone rocks that dominate the Clare landscape provide one of the most fascinating natural anomalies Ireland has to offer. Known as the Burren – meaning 'rocky land' in Gaelic – the area consists of thousands of great limestone slabs or pavements, with deep cracks, known as grikes, between them. This lunar-like landscape is believed to have been created from the skeletons of wildlife that inhabited the area over 300 million years ago.

This amazing plateau appears as though it could support no life, but surprisingly, the Burren is a wilderness of wild plants that have grown up in the cracks between the pavements, many of which can be seen nowhere else in the world, but the Mediterranean and the Alps. The contradiction of these plants surviving side by side has confused botanists for many years. They thrive because, although the land appears

deceptively dry and barren, there flows beneath the limestone myriad streams and rivers. In wet weather these *turloughs*, or seasonal lakes, rise to the surface.

Underneath the Burren lies a complexity of caves and potholes, most of which are inaccessible and unexplored. This unique and amazing landmark is a popular site for visitors who come to admire its strangeness and its marvellous botanical life.

The Giant's Causeway
CO. ANTRIM

This geological phenomenon is believed to have been created sixty million years ago by a process of volcanic eruptions and the cooling of molten lava. Over the millennia, further layers of basalt lava built up, until a curious landmark of near-perfect hexagonal columns on the cliff edge, extending right down into the sea was formed. The thousands of basalt columns range up to over six metres high, and this unusual rocky promontory on the coast of Northern Ireland provides one of the most strange and spectacular sights the country has to offer.

The bizarre structure of the Causeway has made it subject to numerous myths and legends to explain its existence. The most popular tells how the great giant and Ulster warrior Finn McCool, who lived on the headland of Antrim, fell in love with a lady giant who lived on one of the Hebridean islands, Staffa. He was believed to have built the Causeway as a road across the water to see his love. Force is given to this legend by the fact that similar geological curiosities have been found on Staffa.

Bog Cotton
CO. KILDARE

One of Ireland's most famous natural landmarks is its bogs. Slowly formed over thousands of years, two main types of bog or peat land cover about fifteen per cent of the country: the blanket bog is common to the west of Ireland and the raised bog is characteristic of the midlands. These bogs have proved to be a valuable source of information about Ireland's geological history.

The flora and fauna of the bogs are unique and fascinating, being an intrinsic part of the Irish heritage. Bog Myrtle, for example, is often used to flavour drinks, and the Bogbean plant was once used to cure boils. The Bog Cotton shown here is another plant found extensively in the Irish peatland, dotting the landscape with its white balls. The bogs were once much more widespread, but continued use of the peat for fuel and agricultural purposes has meant that they are gradually decreasing, and the unusual plant and animal life that inhabit these bogs may one day be lost forever.

Croagh Patrick
CO. MAYO

The magnificent, awe-inspiring Croagh Patrick towers over the town of Westport and the inlet of Clew Bay, keeping an eternal vigil. This Holy Mountain, named after the Patron Saint of Ireland, stands 765 metres high.

As far back as 3000 BC, the mountain was a site of pagan worship, in honour of the good god of the Celts, Lug. It was transformed to a site of Christian worship after AD 441 when St Patrick is believed to have spent forty days on the mountain fasting and praying like Moses. All year round, pilgrims travel from throughout Ireland to climb the indomitable heights and reach the flat peak, where mass is held, and confessions are heard amongst the low clouds, and there are breathtaking views over the Irish countryside.

The great national pilgrimage to the summit of Croagh Patrick takes place on the last Sunday in July – the same day as the ancient pagan festival of Lug, and is known as Reek Sunday ('Reek' is the local name for the mountain). Pilgrims of old would travel barefoot, and would climb by night, carrying torches and candles to show the way, creating an eerie trail of light up the darkened mountain. Today the pilgrimages are made by both day and night as people come to pay homage to a Saint whose influence remains throughout Ireland.

THE MAGIC OF IRELAND

In its wild countryside and hypnotic rivers, its elegant architecture and spell-binding relics, Ireland is a magical land. Every element of the country combines to create an enchanting beauty that can be found nowhere else in the world.

Laragh
CO. WICKLOW

The county of Wicklow has been unofficially, but justly, dubbed 'the Garden of Ireland'. Lying just a short way from Dublin, the change in atmosphere is quite breathtaking. From the hustle and bustle of one of the busiest capitals in Europe, to a wilderness of beauty and solitude. The Wicklow mountains cover much of the county and are a spectacular landmark: high granite outcrops, rough and grey with a wild beauty, complement the lushness of the fields and countryside which lie at their feet. Within a small area, it is possible to see the Irish landscape at its harshest, and its most delicate.

Scattered amidst the scenery are numerous small villages, unaffected by their proximity to Dublin, and quaintly old-fashioned in their aspect and pace of life. Laragh, pictured here, is one of the most picturesque: the kind of village naturally associated with traditional Irish culture; with thatched cottages and locals simply passing the time of day. Wicklow is a patchwork of wooded areas, of hills and fields and of sparkling lakes, an undisturbed tranquillity, with a landscape that is unlikely to have changed since the Celts ruled Ireland.

Horses
CO. KILDARE

Kildare is the very soul of horse country in Ireland. The small hills and flat plains that typify this area not far from Dublin, are ideal for the breeding and training of the thoroughbreds of which the Irish are so proud. The main area for this is the Curragh – the home of the Irish Derby, possibly the most famous and popular race of many in the country. In Kildare town, the National Stud farm is a great attraction and manifests everything that this county is about. This bloodstock farm was founded at the turn of the century, by the somewhat eccentric Colonel William Walker. His success, he claimed, relied upon the astrological signs of his horses, and he would devotedly plot the charts of his new foals, and sell them accordingly. Bizarre though this seems, it appears to have worked.

The mild Irish climate has meant that horses, both wild and hand-reared, have thrived in the countryside. The flat lands of Kildare are made up of a layer of lush grass covering a rocky limestone surface, which provides essential calcium for the horses.

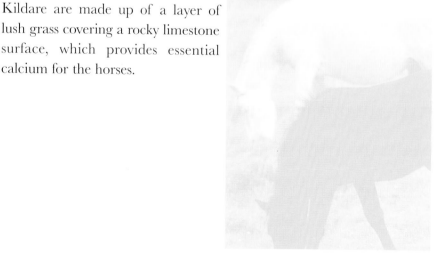

The Glen of Imaal
CO. WICKLOW

The darkening skies over this part of Co. Wicklow add to the wild and fantastic atmosphere that hangs over the Glen of Imaal much of the time. The area is dominated by the black and purple, austere but impressive peak of Lugnaquilla, the highest mountain in the Wicklow range. The Wicklows have a history of being a great hide-out for those in trouble with the law, since the days of the invasions; their great stretch of daunting rocks proving an untempting prospect for those in pursuit, and nearly impossible to master.

The Glen of Imaal is one of the more untamed parts of Wicklow, and is a small but fascinating place to visit for the scenery alone. Its other claim to fame is the breed of terrier known as the Glen of Imaal terrier, which originated in this area. In this photograph, a man and his dog drive the cattle home, against a backdrop of hills disappearing into the foreboding evening sky.

The River Shannon
CO. OFFALY

The Shannon is by far the longest river in Ireland, indeed it is longer than any other in the British Isles. It begins its journey in the majestic slopes of the Cuilcagh Mountain, and meanders its way through 250 miles of Irish countryside along the shores of Longford, Westmeath and Offaly to the Atlantic Ocean between Loop Head and Kerry Head. The Shannon itself, and the countryside through which it flows is home to a diverse selection of wildlife, plants and birds.

The river is largely made up of a chain of lakes through the heart of Ireland, including Loughs Allen, Ree and Derg. The significance of the Shannon to the Irish is both symbolic and practical. In ancient times, the river represented the division between Leinster and Connacht; and castles and monasteries — such as the settlement at Clonmacnoise shown here — were built along its shores. Today, the river is the source of Ireland's hydro-electric power, from a station based near Limerick; it also provides the major part of the country's water-based tourist trade.

Evening at Clonmacnoise
CO. OFFALY

In Ireland's cities, the evening is the time when the streets come alive. The increasing number of young people in the country means that socialising has become more important, and pubs and bars in the busier areas are packed with Ireland's youth, creating a pleasant and lively atmosphere. In rural areas, however, the customs of old times still exist, and the evening is the time to catch a glimpse of an Ireland most people find familiar through books and pictures. After a day's work farming, the men still frequently gather in pairs or groups in the solitary peacefulness of the countryside. Here they sit quietly indulging in the age-old Irish passion for 'spinning a yarn', chatting and passing away the early evening in a slow and contented way. An occupation typical of the peoples' laid-back attitude. Despite contemporary pastimes, the unhurried pace of life that has characterised the Irish for centuries is still evident.

Here at Clonmacnoise, the ancient monastic settlement in Co. Offaly, reigns a peace and serenity suited to this way of life and custom. As the sun sets over the scattered grave slabs and crosses, local men watch a scene that has changed little since pre-Christian times.

Phoenix Park
CO. DUBLIN

Phoenix Park is the largest enclosed park in Europe. It lies in Dublin and spans 1752 acres. Some of this is beautifully landscaped gardens, and other parts are a wilderness of plantlife and trees, home to a number of birds and animals that are rarely seen within city walls. There are over 300 species of plants and ferns to be found here, and the park has become a sanctuary for rare birds.

The park was founded in 1662 by the Duke of Ormonde, and was originally a deer enclosure. The fallow deer have been inhabitants here since that time, and are just one of the many attractions to be found in this remarkable area. The park was opened to the public in 1745 by Lord Chesterfield, and further developments and improvements were made in the nineteenth century by Decimus Burton. The park now incorporates a zoological garden, nature trails through the acres of wild land, sports fields for hurling and polo and a range of interesting monuments. The enclosures of the park also house a number of buildings, including the Irish President's official residence. Phoenix Park is an unexpected haven not far from Dublin's thriving city centre.

Cottage on the Blasket Islands
CO. KERRY

This deserted cottage is one of the relics of a hardy people who lived on the Blasket Islands, at the end of the Dingle Peninsula. The ruins of the cottages that once housed a thriving community, fighting hard to survive against the harsh climates of the Blaskets, are now a poignant addition to the rocky, splintered promontories that make up the seven islands.

The main industry on the islands was fishing, due to the wealth of sealife available in the waters surrounding the Blaskets. The population of the islands reached its peak in the 1840s, as more and more starving people infiltrated from the mainland where famine was taking hold. Emigration meant that by the mid-twentieth century, there were just a few families left on the larger islands, and by 1953 they were all but deserted.

Today there is nothing left of this period of relative affluence other than the slowly decaying cottages – evocative relics of happier times. The Blaskets are, however, a mysterious and fascinating place, their very solitude increasing the magical atmosphere.

Dingle
CO. KERRY

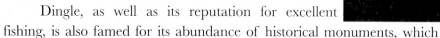

O n the edge of the sea, surrounded by the long grasses, men would sit and pass the evening in pleasant chatter and silence, appreciating the beauty of their land. This is a tradition that is still maintained, and will be as long as there is such beauty to appreciate. Here at Dingle, once a remote, Gaelic-speaking town, but now a busier fishing port, there are still places to find to be alone.

Dingle, as well as its reputation for excellent fishing, is also famed for its abundance of historical monuments, which

include high crosses, a plethora of standing stones, ruins of churches, whole colonies of beehive houses and holy wells. It is also home to the Gallarus Oratory, a sandstone chapel, that is still in almost perfect condition. They all add a majestic, ancient air to an area that becomes a curious and very Irish mixture of the ancient and the contemporary. They are as much a part of the Dingle landscape and heritage as the hills and the sea that surround it.

Morning Light on Reeds, Innisfree
CO. SLIGO

Lying in the grand Lough Gill, the small Isle of Innisfree has become a Mecca for W. B. Yeats fans all over the world. Yeats himself has association with many places in County Sligo, and particularly around the Lough. Dooney Rock is the place where Yeats sat and gained much of his inspiration, gazing across the Lough, affected by the beauty of the spot and the romantic islands that are scattered around it. And at Dromahair, a beautiful little village with views across Lough Gill, he penned his poem 'The Man who Dreamed of Faeryland'.

There is an air of fantasy that hangs over Lough Gill, enhanced by its surrounding fairytale woodland, and unsurpassed scenery. Innisfree particularly is a place of magic, when the light shines on its uninhabited land, reflecting off the waters of the Lough. A silver bell from a nearby Dominican monastery was thrown into its waters many centuries ago, and one of the legends that surround this magical place says that you can still hear it toll from deep in the waters, but only if you are pure of heart.

Late Evening
CO. LIMERICK

Limerick is often passed over in favour of the more dramatic landscapes of surrounding counties, but it has its own charms and beauty. Its boundary in the north is the Shannon river, and as such it is a fertile land, rich with lush pastures and gently rolling hills. It is a largely agricultural region, producing crops of potatoes and oats, and also boasting a flourishing industry of dairy farming.

The land is flat, and chequered with dry-stone walls, forming acres of rich pasture land and neat fields. Geologically, it could not be more different from the wild rocky landscape of Co. Clare which lies just to the north. It is this abrupt geological diversity that makes Ireland so fascinating and appealing, as a short walk can take a visitor to what seems like a whole new country.

The county is sparsely populated and the farmland unbroken, except for a few villages or the odd house on the landscape; because of this it has remained unspoilt for many years. It is a farmers' region, where a hard day's toil is rewarded by peace and reflection, in the midst of the beautiful countryside.

Fishing Boats
CO. GALWAY

Galway began its life as a fishing community and has continued this tradition into the twentieth century. Set between the banks of the rushing River Corrib, and the wild Atlantic Ocean, men have made their living in this way for centuries. The fishing community were the first to inhabit this area of Galway, and because of its location on the waterfront, the place has many associations with the water both in legend and fact.

Galway became Ireland's third maritime port, and struck up strong trading associations with the Spanish, who would deliver cargoes of wine into the Bay. Fishing eventually became a secondary industry, as increasing numbers of traders and merchants came to seek their fortunes here at what became the hub of trade and imports.

The Old Quays still bear evidence of this water-based heritage, in the form of the Spanish Arch. This was the site of the old docks, where the Spanish would have unloaded their cargoes. Built in 1584, it was designed to protect the harbour which, at the time, was outside the boundaries of the city.

Ireland Past and Present

Created by W. Blaeu, this incredibly detailed map of Ireland dates from 1635. By AD 1000, the country was divided into four distinct areas, the boundaries of which can be seen here. To the north is Ulster, the east Leinster, the south Munster and the west Connacht. In ancient times the Kings and Chieftains of these areas fought bitterly for dominance.

Although the spellings and boundaries of some of the counties may have changed slightly, many remain similar to the way they were centuries ago. The exception is Co. Wicklow, once part of the counties of Meath, Caterlagh and Wexford on this map. Detailed below are the modern counties with their sixteenth-century names, followed by the page numbers on which locations are featured in this book.

Co. Carlow (*Caterlagh*)
144

Co. Clare (*Clare*)
17, 22, 75, 81, 121, 129, 145, 147, 156, 162, 177, 178

Co. Cork (*Corck*)
61, 96, 105, 106, 140

Co. Dublin (*Dublyn*)
54, 57, 58, 59, 60, 62, 63, 65, 66, 73, 92, 97, 99, 103, 104, 107, 109, 110, 111, 159, 164, 168, 169, 174, 190

Co. Donegal (*Dunghall*)
28, 30, 43, 47, 72, 76, 119, 133, 136

Co. Galway (*Galway*)
16, 20, 34, 40, 42, 46, 48, 74, 77, 80, 83, 87, 93, 100, 108, 118, 122, 125, 126, 132, 154, 155, 158, 160, 161, 165, 195

Co. Kerry (*Kerry*)
38, 51, 82, 84, 85, 88, 98, 117, 124, 127, 128, 134, 142, 152, 153, 163, 167, 176, 191, 192

Co. Kildare (*Kildare*)
56, 180, 186

Co. Kilkenny (*Killkenny*)
18, 19, 26, 150

Co. Leitrim (*Letrim*)
41

Co. Limerick (*Lymericke*)
194

Co. Louth (*Louth*)
137, 175

Co. Mayo (*Mayo*)
44, 50, 78, 89, 114, 181

Co. Meath (*Meath*)
146

Co. Offaly (*Queenes County*)
27, 32, 116, 138, 139, 188, 189

Co. Sligo (*Slego*)
49, 70, 86, 141, 193

Co. Tipperary (*Typerary*)
24, 120, 166

Co. Waterford (*Waterford*)
25

Co. Westmeath (*Meath*)
123

Co. Wicklow (incorporated into areas of *Dublyn*, *Meath* and *Caterlagh*)
21, 45, 157, 184, 187

Co. Antrim *(Antrim)*
35, 67, 102, 179

Co. Armagh *(Armagh)*
14

Co. Down *(Doune)*
33

Co. Fermanagh *(Fermanagh)*
29, 31, 64, 172

Co. Tyrone (*Upper Tyrone* and *Nether Tyrone*)
90

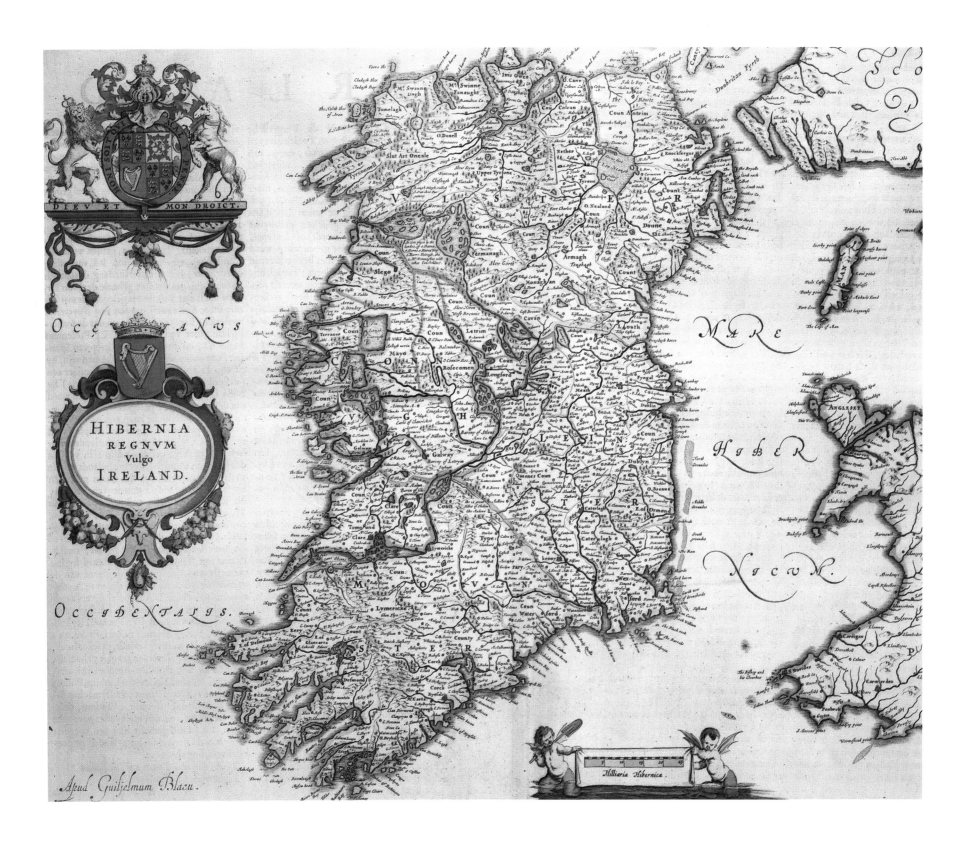

Index

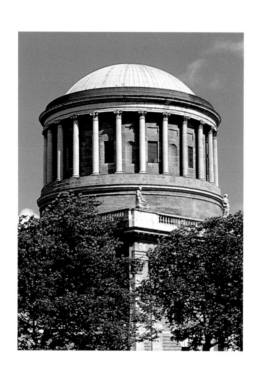